FORWARD

A SMALL GROUP JOURNEY TOWARD A FULL LIFE IN CHRIST

FORWARD

A Small Group Journey Toward
a Full Life in Christ

Nick Cunningham

Abingdon Press / Nashville

Forward
A Small Group Journey Toward a Full Life in Christ

Copyright © 2017 Abingdon Press
All rights reserved.

This book is printed on elemental chlorine-free paper.

978-1-5018-3746-3

17 18 19 20 21 22 23 24 25 26 — 10 9 8 7 6 5 4 3 2 1
MANUFACTURED IN THE UNITED STATES OF AMERICA

CONTENTS

Introduction

I n life there is no neutral.

My grandpa Flack lived on a lake, and he had one of those paddleboats that you would power with your legs. My cousins and I would take it out and explore the cove around the corner from my grandpa's property. More often than not, our adventures would escalate into a crisis that required a daring rescue attempt by one of the uncles. Either we would drift too far out into the open water, or we would get the boat tangled up in some weeds, or—the most exciting thing—we would manage to flip it over.

Paddleboats are not the easiest things to get around in. For one thing, you have to steer it with that little lever in between the seats, so they don't exactly handle very well. Your only options are either a hard turn to the right or a hard turn to the left—so you'd better mean it when you push that lever.

At the same time, there is no such thing as neutral when you are in a paddleboat. Sitting still is not an option. Because of the waves and water currents, even when you aren't trying to get anywhere you are still heading *somewhere*. The only way to get somewhere on purpose is to paddle deliberately in the direction you want to go. And because of the archaic steering mechanism, you will more than likely have to circle back around a couple of times in order to finally reach your destination.

In life, there is no such thing as neutral. Just as in a paddleboat, even when we are not trying to get anywhere we are still headed *somewhere*. It's easy to believe that we can put life on hold and one day get around to straightening things out, but it doesn't work that way. Whether we are meaning to or not, we are all making decisions, or not making decisions, that impact our trajectory and shape our lives in various ways. We're either paddling in a direction we choose, or we're drifting in the direction the waves happen to carry us.

Bottom line: We are all headed somewhere and we are all becoming someone. The question is, are we headed where we want to go and becoming who we want to be?

I bring this up because of the good news at the heart of the Christian faith. There is, of course, the good news of God's complete and total forgiveness for all of the ways we have blown it. In Jesus, our sins have been taken care of. However, there is also some more good news. We can be transformed. Not only does the gospel declare the truth of God's forgiveness but it also speaks of the possibility of a new life that we can live right now.

You and I, because of God's grace and through the power of the Holy Spirit, can change.

We don't have to be a victim to the waves or just drift around aimlessly. The gospel declares that we can actually move forward. One of my favorite passages of Scripture can be found in Second Corinthians 3. In this passage (verse 18), Paul says that those of us who have said yes to the saving love of God are being transformed through the power of the Holy Spirit into the very likeness of Christ "with ever-increasing glory" (NIV). Transformed into the likeness of Christ with ever-increasing glory. I would call that moving forward.

James 1:4 says that the goal of our faith is that we would be mature: "Let this endurance complete its work so that you may be fully mature, complete, and lacking in nothing." I'll be honest. I'm not a huge fan of that word *mature*. It sounds so stiff and even snobby. When I hear that word I immediately think of a girl named Tiffany—someone I went to middle school with who always used to say to me, "You are so immature, when are you ever going to grow up?" I mean if maturity is about being all stiff and snobby, then I don't want anything to do with it. But that isn't what the author of James is talking about. He goes on to define what he means by explaining that maturity is about being whole—it's about being complete—specifically, "lacking in nothing." Spiritual maturity is really a matter of growing into who we really are.

The good news isn't just about what happens after we die—it's also about what is possible right now on this side of death. Jesus believes that it is possible for us to live a really beautiful life. I'm not sure how many of us actually know, let alone believe, this is possible.

Many of us have been made to think that salvation is simply a one-time decision and transaction between you and God, which assures you of a blissful afterlife. When this becomes the totality of what many in the church believe about salvation, then it's no wonder the church often seems just as greedy, just as addicted, just as insecure, and just as relationally bankrupt as the rest of the world. In this mind-set, the only difference is that we will get to go to heaven after we die—and so the life of faith becomes about simply enduring. Just hold on and wait to die.

I don't know about you, but that doesn't exactly do anything for me. That doesn't get me out of bed in the morning. That doesn't sound like something worth giving my life to. That certainly doesn't sound like something that honors God and proves to people that Jesus is who he says he is.

The good news of Jesus Christ isn't just about what happens after we die; it is also about what is possible now. Because of Jesus we don't have to fear death, and at the same time we don't have to fear life either. We don't have to drift through life being tossed about by the wind and the waves. We can be changed; we can be mature; we can move forward.

Now if you are anything like me, then you have what I like to call a *maturity gap*. There is a distance, a maturity gap if you will, between our ideal self and our real self. There is a distance between who we want to be, or who we know we could be, and who we are. There is a gap between the life that we want to live and the life that we do live, and it bothers us. We all live with some sense of frustration about that maturity gap. For some it's more profound and obvious than others, but we all live with some sense of frustration with the distance between our ideal and our real. So the question is, how do we close that gap? How do we push ahead and shorten or even eliminate that distance? What is it going to take for us to start living forward?

That's what this book is about. We are going to spend our time in a truly fascinating passage at the beginning of Second Peter. This passage is loaded with insights on what it means to grow in maturity. At the heart of it is a list of seven virtues—goodness, knowledge, self-control, perseverance, godliness, mutual affection, and love— all rooted in faith in the power and promises of God in Jesus Christ. These virtues are not a list of what God wants *from* us, but a list of what God wants *for* us. This list is not an exhaustive description of what a life of maturity looks like, and I don't think the author intends for us to believe we have to grow in these virtues in the order in which they are found in this passage. Instead, the author wants us to know that because of what God has made available to us in Jesus, these virtues are possible. We are going to spend a session on each one of these virtues, because they serve in a way as directional markers in our effort to live a life of forward movement.

This book is also meant to be a follow-up study to the *One* curriculum, which is all about fully embracing our shared life in Christ.[1] In that study I offer that authentic Christ-centered community does not happen on its own, but it is intentionally built and carefully sustained around three core practices: pushing one another forward, lifting one another up, and sending one another out. This book is a deeper look at that first core practice: pushing one another forward. A fair question to ask is, "Pushing one another forward toward what exactly?" My hope is that this book can help answer that question and offer you a resource in your commitment to wanting more for one another.

Because in life there is no neutral.

A life lived well is a life lived on purpose.

A life lived with direction.

A life lived forward.

Session 1
Goodness

The summer after my senior year of high school, two of my best friends and I took a trip up to Wisconsin before we all went off to college. One of my friend's grandparents owned a cabin on a beautiful lake way up in the northern part of the state. We stayed at their cabin that week and had a blast. We fished. We water-skied. We went hiking. It was such a great time.

We wanted to squeeze every last drop out of that week before we had to leave, so we decided to spend the entire last day out on the lake and start the drive home later that evening. This meant we would have to drive home through the night, and we would arrive really early the next morning. The drive was ridiculous—I want to say it was around twelve hours or something, all at night. But there were three of us and we decided we would all take shifts. One guy would sleep, one guy would drive, and the other guy would make sure that the driver stayed awake.

We started the trip back home around seven or eight o'clock at night. I took the first shift driving, and one of the others volunteered to be the first sleeper. He said he could go ahead and grab a nap so he would be ready to drive a bit later. Well, eight hours later that joker was still sleeping! As hard as we tried, we could not get him to wake up—and believe me, two college-age guys on a road trip can think of some pretty creative ways to try to wake someone up.

When he finally did wake up, it was early the next morning and he felt horrible for sleeping all through the night. But because he was feeling quite rested—and we were exhausted—he said he could finish the drive alone and we could both get some sleep. No need for the keep-the-driver-awake shift. We took him up on the offer, and while "sleeping beauty" went into a gas station to get some coffee we both fell right to sleep. Now I happen to be a fairly large guy, which means that I don't get along very well with tight spaces. I didn't sleep well in the car. I managed to sleep only a couple of hours before I woke up. Turns out, that was a really good thing, because when I woke up, I discovered that my friend had been driving the entire time in the wrong direction.

Two hours. In the wrong direction.

Of course, like all good friends, we never let him live that one down. I don't think he ever drove again on any of our road trips.

There's a lesson in this funny story. You see, we can be right on track when it comes to our intended destination, but all out of whack when it comes to our current direction. My sleeping friend had every intention of getting us home. The only problem was that his direction was all wrong. Where we want to go and where we are presently headed are not always the same thing.

Called and Equipped to Move Forward

There's an important passage in Second Peter that can help us go in the right direction, showing us the goal of spiritual maturity and important signposts as we move toward it. In 2 Peter 1:3-11, the author lists seven virtues, all grounded in faith: moral excellence (goodness), knowledge, self-control, endurance (perseverance), godliness, affection for others (mutual affection), and love (verses 5-7). We'll be spending a lot of time in this passage throughout this study, because there's so much we can learn from it. Here is what the author has to say:

> [3]By his divine power the Lord has given us everything we need for life and godliness through the knowledge of the one who called us by his own honor and glory. [4]Through his honor and glory he has given us his precious and wonderful promises, that you may share the divine nature and escape from the world's immorality that sinful craving produces.

⁵This is why you must make every effort to add moral excellence to your faith; and to moral excellence, knowledge; ⁶and to knowledge, self-control; and to self-control, endurance; and to endurance, godliness; ⁷and to godliness, affection for others; and to affection for others, love. ⁸If all these are yours and they are growing in you, they'll keep you from becoming inactive and unfruitful in the knowledge of our Lord Jesus Christ. ⁹Whoever lacks these things is shortsighted and blind, forgetting that they were cleansed from their past sins.

¹⁰Therefore, brothers and sisters, be eager to confirm your call and election. Do this and you will never ever be lost. ¹¹In this way you will receive a rich welcome into the everlasting kingdom of our Lord and savior Jesus Christ. (2 Peter 1:3-11)

The author of Second Peter makes it clear right from the beginning of the passage that we have been called and equipped, and we are now expected to be moving forward with Christian virtue growing within us. In verse 3, we are told that God's divine power has given us everything we need to live a godly life. Just to be sure, that word for *everything* literally means . . . everything.

Everything we need to live a life of forward movement, we already have. I really like how he puts it in verse 4. The author says that through God's precious promises, you and I may "share the divine nature." Share the divine nature. It's clear that this author has a great deal of confidence when it comes to the quality of life and the depth of character that is possible for a disciple of Jesus Christ.

In Jesus, we have been given everything we need—say it with me—EVERYTHING we need to move forward in life. And moving forward means nothing less than sharing in the divine nature. However, all of us have what I call a "maturity gap." There is a distance between our ideal and our real—between who we currently are and who we could be. So the question becomes, how do we close the gap? How do we move forward?

Grounded in Faith

Let's go back to Second Peter. Before we get into moral excellence or goodness, the first virtue the author lists, let's take a look at the phrase that gets it all started. In verse 5 the author says, "For this very reason, make every effort to add to your faith…" (NIV). Faith, my friends, is where a life of forward movement begins. Faith is what makes possible all that comes after it; faith opens the door to all of the other virtues that come next in the passage. Apart from a faith that is rooted in the truth of who Jesus has revealed God to be, and what God has accomplished through Jesus—these virtues, this life of forward movement, is nothing more than a pipe dream.

Closing our maturity gap is way more than simple behavior modification—it is character transformation. It isn't just about getting rid of a few bad habits—it is about becoming what the Scriptures call a new creation, being transformed from the inside out. That is what faith is all about. In fact, a way to understand our faith is that it's our inner life: the aspect of our lives that undergirds everything else and gives us meaning, direction, and purpose. And so if we are going to experience any sort of change or get any sort of forward momentum, cultivating our faith is the place where we will need God to work first and foremost.

There is an interesting encounter with Jesus in the Gospels of Mark and Luke that illustrates the fundamental role faith plays in our lives:

[1]After a few days, Jesus went back to Capernaum, and people heard that he was at home. [2]So many gathered that there was no longer space, not even near the door. Jesus was speaking the word to them. [3]Some people arrived, and four of them were bringing to him a man who was paralyzed. [4]They couldn't carry him through the crowd, so they tore off part of the roof above where Jesus was. When they had made an opening, they lowered the mat on which the paralyzed man was lying. [5]When Jesus saw their faith, he said to the paralytic, "Child, your sins are forgiven!"

[6]Some legal experts were sitting there, muttering among themselves, [7]"Why does he speak this way? He's insulting God. Only the one God can forgive sins."

[8]Jesus immediately recognized what they were discussing, and he said to them, "Why do you fill your minds with these questions? [9]Which is easier—to say to a paralyzed person, 'Your sins are forgiven,' or to say, 'Get up, take up your bed, and

walk'? [10]But so you will know that the Human One has authority on the earth to forgive sins"—he said to the man who was paralyzed, [11]"Get up, take your mat, and go home."

[12]Jesus raised him up, and right away he picked up his mat and walked out in front of everybody. They were all amazed and praised God, saying, "We've never seen anything like this!"

(Mark 2:1-12; see Luke 5:17-26)

In this passage, Jesus is teaching in a home and this huge crowd comes to hear him. A couple of men try to get their paralyzed friend to Jesus because they had heard about what he could do, but the crowd is so big that they can't get into the house. So they decide to do the most sensible thing: They dig a hole in the roof and lower their friend on a mat right in front of Jesus. Now there are so many things about this story that I love, but there is one thing that is strange—uncomfortable at first. Jesus looks at this paralyzed man and the first thing he says to him is, "Child, your sins are forgiven!" (Mark 2:5).

Can you imagine what this man's friends were thinking? "Wait, what? 'Your sins are forgiven'? We didn't carry him all the way here and dig a hole in this roof so you could tell him that his sins are forgiven." What about the man on the mat? "That's nice. I'm forgiven, but I still can't walk. When are you going to do something about that?" Well, a few verses later we see that Jesus does eventually do something about that; he heals the man (verses 9-12). But by offering forgiveness first, Jesus reveals to us our deepest need in life: to have our sins forgiven, to be set right with God, our Creator. In other words, to have our inner life made well. I don't believe Jesus is suggesting that the root of paralysis is personal sin. He speaks against this sort of worldview in John 9 with the man born blind (John 9:3). But what Jesus communicates in this passage is that the greatest thing God can do for us is to not fix something about us, but it's to fix us, to heal us at our core. That's what faith is all about. It's a matter of entrusting ourselves to the saving love of God and allowing the truth of the gospel to inform our understanding of who we are and how we are to live.

When it comes to our maturity gap and all the ways we are failing to live a life of forward movement, we must be careful not to get hung up on the symptoms without addressing the sickness. The greatest thing God can do for us is not to change something about us, but to change us—to make us into the right kind of people. This takes discipline on our part to realize that here at the beginning, but then also to continue to recognize it from here on out. Our first step in addressing any sort of maturity gap is not to plan or strategize, to go and listen to a sermon, to read a blog, or to get some advice. Our first step always ought to be to fall back into the good news of the gospel, to ground ourselves in the saving love of God.

At the same time, we also have to understand that faith is what allows us to tap into God's power to bring about all sorts of change within us. The trick is staying connected to it. When I was in college, I served as a youth pastor in South Carolina. One year my roommates and I got into a prank war with a group of high school boys. Now for the most part the so-called "war" was pretty lopsided, because we straight-up owned them. However, they did manage, just one time, to get us pretty good. One Wednesday night while we were all at the church for an event, the power went out for a few minutes and then it came back on. No big deal. Well, when my roommates and I got home, we discovered that the power was still out at our house. So we sat around for a while in the dark, doing homework by candlelight while we waited for the power to be restored. After a few hours, I went into my bedroom and flipped on the light switch out of habit. Then something strange happened: The ceiling fan started to move. I thought this was odd, and so I reached up and twisted one of the light bulbs to see what would happen. Sure enough, it lit up. I kid you not. These high school boys had gotten into our house and unscrewed every single light bulb and unplugged everything electric from its socket. While we sat around for hours thinking the power was out, the power had been there the whole time. It was available, but the connection to it was broken.

The author of Second Peter tells us that God's divine power has already given us everything we need to live a godly life (2 Peter 1:3). The question is, are we staying connected to it? That's why this list begins with faith—with our inner life—with staying connected to the divine power that has been made available to us in Jesus.

You see, the gospel doesn't begin as something that we do. Of course, it does involve what we do, but it doesn't start as something that we do. The gospel begins as a life-giving announcement about what God has already done. In light of this we ought to be in the habit of preaching the gospel to ourselves every single day, a thousand times a day if need be. In a way, moving forward actually begins with regularly going backward: back to the cross, back to the gospel, back to the saving love of God and the life-altering truth of what Jesus has made available to us. Of course we are called to move forward, to grow, to become more than we have been. But if we aren't living from the inside out and if we aren't constantly grounding ourselves in the gospel, then we will never make it because whatever power is moving us forward will turn out to be something other than the gospel. Whether that power is willpower or maybe self-righteousness, no matter what it is, it's something less than the gospel and we will never make it.

Goodness

Now that we have established the importance of being grounded in faith, I think we are safe to start exploring the virtues that we find next in Second Peter, and the role they play in moving us forward. In verse 5 the author says to us, "This is why you must make every effort to add moral excellence to your faith...." The word for moral excellence in the original language of the New Testament is the ancient Greek word *arête*. It can also be translated as virtue (ESV) or goodness (NRSV). The word *goodness* is a great translation of that word, because it captures the simple yet ideal virtue that the author envisions. It means something like excellence of character, uncommon civic virtue, or character worthy of praise—everything true goodness might entail. This, my friends, is what you call a loaded word. The author is borrowing this word from the surrounding culture. Even though the world, at the time, was ruled by Rome politically, it was still very much under the influence of ancient Greek philosophy. In Greek thought, arête was a highly prized virtue and a goal of all Greek education. We might understand it to mean something like "the highest quality of excellence." How do you like that? Bottom line, arête is as good as it gets. Goodness is life in perfect balance—it's humanity running on all cylinders. This word isn't used very often in the New Testament, and actually this is the only time it is ascribed to human beings. In verse 3 the author used the word to describe God's own "glory," that is, God's excellence that is worthy of praise.

Whoa. Not exactly easing into it, huh? Because of God's excellence, we are challenged to our own excellence. This mirrors what we said above, which we found in verse 4: Because of what God has accomplished in and through Jesus, human beings can come to share God's own nature. For the author of Second Peter, that begins with goodness in response to God's goodness.

Now this, of course, echoes much of what has already been said, but I want to park here for a bit and here's why: I think that one of the biggest reasons why many of us struggle to experience the reality of our salvation—to move forward—isn't because we don't have a big enough sense of who God is. Instead, it's because we don't have a big enough sense of who God thinks we can be. It's not that we don't have a high enough view of divinity—it's that we have too low a view of humanity.

Sadly, a lot of this comes from religious voices we have in our heads, which makes it seem like the only way to respond to a holy God is to feel really awful about yourself. Many of us who grew up in the church grew up hearing something like this: "God is really good and holy, and you are really wicked and evil, and if you don't constantly feel terrible about that then you don't get it." It's often made to seem like God wants nothing more than for us to feel guilty and shameful about all of the ways we fall short.

In fact, I'm sure that many of us felt really uncomfortable reading the lines just up above: "Because of what God has accomplished in and through Jesus, human beings can come to share God's own nature." I'll be honest, I felt uncomfortable typing them. It doesn't feel humble enough. It feels like we are getting a little too comfortable being a human, and if we are doing this whole Jesus thing right then we shouldn't be content with being a human.

Biblical scholar N. T. Wright sums up this tension quite well in his commentary on this passage:

> [God] wants nothing less for us than that we should come to share his own very nature (verse 4). Some Christians have felt uneasy about this idea, as though the humility to which we are so often exhorted ought to stop us short from thinking of actually sharing God's very being or nature. Others, though (particularly in the Eastern Christian traditions), have seen this as central to what it means to be a Christian. After all, if we say that the holy spirit is fully divine, and if we say that the holy spirit comes to live within us and transform us from within, what is that but to say that the divine nature is already dwelling within us, leading us forward until we are suffused with God's own presence and power?[1]

(As good as that is, it sounds even better when you imagine him saying it in his British accent.)

Not long ago, I got an e-mail from a guy letting me have it for not talking about sin enough in my messages. In his mind, he thought it was my job as the preacher to make sure that people knew they were sinners. I have a feeling that most, if not all of us, are very much aware of that. We know we're sinners without frequent reminders.

Now hear me when I say this: I wholeheartedly believe that sin is a big deal and that we must take it seriously. But sin is not the point of our story—it certainly isn't the point of God's story. Someone once pointed out to me that the Bible does not begin with sin, and it doesn't end with sin either. The Scriptures begin in Genesis 1 and 2 with God making human beings in God's own image and everything is good—everything is right; everything is as it should be. Of course, then Genesis 3 happens and everything goes haywire; but the Scriptures do not end there. Instead they end with Revelation 21 and 22, with God bringing together heaven and earth—and once again everything is as it should be.

So yes, sin is a big deal, but it isn't the point of our story. The dangerous thing about making it the point of the story is that you then reduce the gospel to simply reminding people of what they already know—that they aren't good enough, that they are a mess. It's all about who they aren't, and that doesn't have the power to change anyone or anything. Instead, if you understand the gospel is aiming for arête—moral excellence or goodness—then it becomes about telling people who they truly are. We are human beings capable of excellence, and God wants to empower us to live out of our true identity. Add goodness to your faith, the author of Second Peter writes, *because it's within your reach*. Because of God's power and excellence, you can strive for virtue and exceptional character as an attainable goal. Now, that has the power to change everything. Maybe that is why it's called the good news.

We see this idea from Jesus over and over again all throughout the Gospels. Often when Jesus heals someone, do you know what he says to them right after? He says to them, "Your faith has saved you" or "Your faith has healed you" (see Mark 5:34; Luke 7:50; 18:42). In fact, one of my favorite encounters with Jesus happens in Mark 5. Jesus is surrounded by a huge crowd of people, and there is this woman who we are told has been subject to bleeding for twelve years. She has exhausted all of her resources in trying to find a remedy, and instead of getting better she has gotten worse. But she's heard of this Jesus and she knows that if she can just touch the edge of his cloak, she touch the edge of his cloak, she could be healed. So she works her way through the crowd, and she is able to reach out and touch just the edge of his cloak and immediately she is healed. The sickness is taken away. Jesus knows right away that something has happened and he stops and asks, "Who touched my clothes?" (Mark 5:30) The disciples think he is crazy because he is surrounded by this huge crowd of people and he wants to know who touched him. "Um, that would be everyone, Jesus." But, you see, Jesus knows that something even more profound needs to happen than just a physical healing.

Eventually the woman realizes that Jesus isn't going to let her sneak away, so she comes up to Jesus and falls at his feet. He says to her, "Daughter, your faith has healed you; go in peace, healed of your disease" (Mark 5:34).

Now my question is, why did Jesus do that? If all that mattered was that she understood that Jesus was the source of her healing—that she was busted and broken and couldn't fix herself—then Jesus could have just let her sneak away. Because let's be honest, that was obvious. She knew she needed Jesus, otherwise she wouldn't have touched his cloak. There was something else that she needed to know. Jesus went out of his way to make sure that she knew her faith was involved in what had just happened. This was an act of empowerment on Jesus' part. He wanted her to know that when her faith connected with his power, unbelievable things could happen.

I believe Jesus wants you to know the same thing. When your faith is combined with God's saving love, it has the potential to accomplish unbelievable things. Now, it's important to not read too much into this. It doesn't mean that every time a prayer isn't answered or a healing doesn't happen that we have a lack of faith—that is a mystery. But the one thing that we can take away from this is that through the saving love of God, Jesus believes that we can live a really beautiful life—that we can experience arête.

There are two questions we need to ask ourselves in light of this. The first one goes like this: "Do you want this?"

Do you want to experience arête—goodness, moral excellence, uncommon virtue?

Do you want to experience the kind of life that is possible in Jesus?

Do you want to be made into the likeness of Christ?

It seems like a silly question, but the truth is we don't automatically answer yes to it. Even though there is this beautiful kind of life offered to us in the gospel, we often settle for less, don't we? Perhaps that is a helpful way for us to think about what sin is—it's all the ways we settle for less than what God wants for us.

Remember, this journey forward—closing our maturity gap—begins with faith. We must depend on God to do in us what we cannot do in ourselves, which requires us to get in touch with our need for God. You and I, we don't like to feel that need or that emptiness, and so we try to drown it out. We try to smother it with all of these temporary fixes that never really satisfy. This is why we go to the computer screen late at night when we are feeling lonely. This is why we give ourselves to people who we know are going to desert us. This is why we look to food, or to substances, or to stuff to try and make us feel somewhat OK—it's an attempt to numb ourselves toward our need for God's work in our lives.

So perhaps how you need to begin your journey forward is with a bit of confession. In what ways have you settled for less than God's own goodness—less than arête? Put a name to your maturity gap. What is it that is separating your ideal from your real?

The second question is just as important and it goes like this: "Do you believe it?"

Do you truly believe that it is possible for you to experience arête?

Do you believe that it is possible for a person to be changed into the likeness of Christ—to share God's own nature?

Do you believe that it is possible for you?

It is so easy to allow those voices of guilt and condemnation to drown out the voice of God, isn't it? I have a friend whose greatest fear is turning out like his father. He is a new father himself, and he lives with this quiet smoldering fear that it is only a matter of time until he makes the same mistakes his father did. I have another friend who constantly gives herself to men who don't love her because she doesn't feel like she deserves anything better. And I have another friend who is really struggling to believe that he will ever know freedom from his addiction. The good news is that we can experience change—knowing arête begins with truly believing that in Jesus, it's possible.

My son Rowan loves to draw. It's one his favorite things to do, but he doesn't like doing it by himself. He wants Daddy to draw with him. So he will hand me a blank piece of paper and a marker and say, "Here, Daddy, draw with me." Because in his mind I can do anything, he usually asks me to draw something really difficult like Optimus Prime or something. Now there are a couple of things that I know I can draw (and none of them are Transformers), so instead I try to talk him into letting me draw one of them instead. But that little guy is persistent . . . and really cute.

It's funny how differently we both see that blank piece of paper. When my son looks at that paper, all he sees is possibility. He sees all of things that it could be. Not me. To me that blank piece of paper is actually quite intimidating. When I look at it I don't see possibility; I see limitations. I don't look at it through the lens of what it could be; I look at it through the lens of what it can't be.

When you look at your life, what do you see? Do you see limitations or do you see possibilities? What have you given up on? What is that thing that you say can't or won't happen? Perhaps what you need to do here as we begin is to ask God to give you the strength to reimagine these things in light of the hope we have in Christ—that in Jesus all things are possible to those who believe. That's what this first virtue, arête, reminds us. We must have faith, and then we must add to that faith goodness, moral excellence, because God has empowered us to achieve nothing less.

In Your Group

Study 2 Peter 1:3-11

Before we go too far, spend some time fam
the passage from 2 Peter 1. Read 2 Peter 1:3-11
and make note of how it hits you. Consider the f
you read it, and answer them in the space provi...u.

1. What do you want to know more about?
2. What about this passage intrigues you?
3. What about this passage challenges you?
4. What about this passage encourages you?
5. How would you summarize this entire passage into one sentence?

y his divine power the Lord has given us everything we need for life and godliness through the knowledge of the one who called us by his own honor and glory. [4]Through his honor and glory he has given us his precious and wonderful promises, that you may share the divine nature and escape from the world's immorality that sinful craving produces.

[5]This is why you must make every effort to add moral excellence to your faith; and to moral excellence, knowledge; [6]and to knowledge, self-control; and to self-control, endurance; and to endurance, godliness; [7]and to godliness, affection for others; and to affection for others, love. [8]If all these are yours and they are growing in you, they'll keep you from becoming inactive and unfruitful in the knowledge of our Lord Jesus Christ. [9]Whoever lacks these things is shortsighted and blind, forgetting that they were cleansed from their past sins.

[10]Therefore, brothers and sisters, be eager to confirm your call and election. Do this and you will never ever be lost. [11]In this way you will receive a rich welcome into the everlasting kingdom of our Lord and savior Jesus Christ.

What Resonates With You?

What from this session resonated with you?

This is a question we are going to ask every week, so it's important to know a bit more about it. There are two sides to this question: Things resonate with us either because they encourage us or because they challenge us.

Challenges are important opportunities to grow toward maturity. Often what we *need* to hear isn't what we *want* to hear, and so our first response to hearing it can be resistance. That's why it's important to pay attention when we feel that resistance, that challenge, because it could be a sign that it's something we need to pay attention to. When you feel yourself bristle at something you come across—when it challenges you—don't ignore it. Poke around a bit and see what's there.

Then there are those moments when we hear something or we read something, and it literally feels like life is being injected into us. It encourages us so powerfully that we feel immediate inspiration. Pay attention to that, too. Grab hold of it. Highlight it, write it down, and be sure to share it with someone else.

These two things are what I mean when I ask how what you read resonated with you. Being able to name it and share it will definitely make your time in this study much more fruitful.

So, what resonated with you? On the following pages, write down the things you encountered in this session that encouraged you and challenged you. The more you can name these things and understand them, the better.

What encouraged you?

What challenged you?

Begin with Faith

Why is it so important for our journey forward to begin with faith? What does faith accomplish for us?

On page 18, I said, "I think that one of the biggest reasons why many of us struggle to experience the reality of our salvation—to move forward—isn't because we don't have a big enough sense of who God is. Instead, it's because we don't have a big enough sense of who God thinks we can be. It's not that we don't have a high enough view of divinity—it's that we have too low a view of humanity."

Do you agree with this statement? Why or why not?

What does this idea have to do with faith?

Goodness

Respond to the two questions that were asked at the end of this session: When it comes to goodness, to arête: Do you want this? And do you believe it?

First, do you want goodness? Even though this is offered to us in Jesus, how have you settled for less?

Second, do you believe it? Do you believe that it is possible, in Jesus, to live a life of goodness? Why or why not? What makes it so hard for us to actually believe it?

The Maturity Gap

In the introduction and in this session, we talked about the maturity gap, the distance between our ideal and our real, who we long to be and who we currently are. What is in your gap? What are some specific things that are keeping you from being who God wants you to be?

Forward Goals

My hope is that over the next several sessions you will be able to develop some goals to help you live a life of forward movement. With the help of your small group, the people who are in this study with you, you can begin to address some of the things in your maturity gap so that you can live a life of forward momentum. Each week you will be challenged to come up with some "Forward Goals" that you can hold one another accountable to. They ought to be action-oriented, specific, and attainable. I'm not here to tell you how you need to respond to all of this. That's what you have one another for. But the purpose is for us actually to move forward and to experience real change. So the goals ought to challenge you, require you to make a change that you can measure and recognize. List two or three goals here, and make a commitment to the others in your small group to hold one another accountable to them. Help one another move forward.

What goals will help you move toward goodness?

Session 2
Knowledge

D o you remember your first serious crush? I do. I remember the first time I saw her in high school—she was a freshman, and I was a sophomore. I was in weight-lifting class and she was in freshmen PE, and whenever she came into the gym all the guys would start showing off. I heard from several people that she thought I was cute. Now, I haven't always been a stunning example of a male specimen—no, no, it's true. I've always been a bit self-conscious about my appearance, and back then my self-consciousness was off the charts. So when all of these people started telling me that this girl wanted me to ask her out, I didn't believe them. I thought they were just trying to get me to embarrass myself. So I did what every guy does who is too afraid to ask a girl out: I flew in under the radar and became her friend. *I'm going to just be her friend*, I thought, *and then maybe she will tell me all about her feelings for me herself.* You know what happened next, right? I got stuck in that awful relationship purgatory known as the "friend zone." After a while she started telling me all about the guys she was crushing on, and calling me when she was heartbroken. We stayed close as friends all through high school and into college. I remember a few nights before I moved down to South Carolina, she told me that she'd had the biggest crush on me for the longest time. I was like, "Say what? Come again?" The kids back in the day weren't lying to me? They were telling me the truth? I spent all that time in the friend zone for nothing?

Now, things worked out just fine for me—I married the love of my life, Lindsey Grayce Jefferies—but this story helps to prove a point. It's one thing to hear a bit of good news, and it's quite another thing to trust it. That intersection of knowing something and trusting it, both understanding it and living as if it's true, is what the author of Second Peter means when he tells us to add knowledge to moral excellence (2 Peter 1:5).

Remember, in living a life of forward movement and in closing our maturity gaps, it all starts with faith. The word for faith in the New Testament can also be translated as trust. It doesn't just mean belief in the truth of something; it means a deep kind of belief that enables trust. It's one thing to hear and mentally believe the good news of Jesus Christ, but it's quite another thing to trust it—to allow it to change the way you see yourself, the way you see others, and the way you live your life.

This brings us to the second virtue that the author mentions in this passage from Second Peter. After instructing us to add to our faith moral excellence, he then goes on to tell us to supplement it with knowledge. And this knowledge is the way in which our faith takes root within us, helping us to see differently and live differently because of our deep trust.

Knowing in the Heart

Greek has several words for knowledge, and the author of Second Peter uses a couple of them in this passage, 2 Peter 1:3-11. In verse 3, the author mentions "the knowledge of the one who called us by his own honor and glory." So in that verse (and also in verse 2), he's talking about the knowledge of God. The Greek word there is *epignosis*, and it sometimes has the sense of recognition or perception. We might think of this as our initial knowledge of God—the moment when we first encounter or recognize the outrageous grace of God. Of course, God is constantly pursuing everyone all the time—this is what United Methodists and others in the Wesleyan tradition call prevenient grace—but there is also a moment of new birth. It's the moment when we first perceive and embrace for ourselves the saving love of God. This moment is what the author of Second Peter is talking about in verses 2 and 3 when he speaks of the knowledge of God.

The knowledge that the author mentions as a virtue in verse 5 refers to what happens after that moment. The word there is *gnosis*;

it's a common Greek word with a wide range of meaning. As it's used here, it means the knowledge that is gradually acquired throughout the faith journey of a disciple of Jesus Christ. Growing in knowledge is essentially how we take in our faith, so to speak. It's about not only hearing the gospel, but it's about learning to trust it more and more as we understand it more completely. This is why Eugene Peterson translates the word in the context of this passage as "spiritual understanding" (THE MESSAGE).

Living a life of forward movement requires us to add knowledge to our faith and goodness—to continually grow in our understanding and confidence of who God is and what the truth of the gospel means for how we live our lives.

This isn't simple head knowledge. If you're anything like me, you usually equate knowledge with information. Information is important, and knowledge involves information. But this sort of knowing isn't just about having the facts straight—it goes beyond that. It's like how we know our favorite song. We don't just know it in our heads—we also know it in our hearts, don't we? It's as if it's always playing somewhere inside of us, and we only have to hear a few notes before we start singing it out loud. Whenever we start to hear it or sing it, the song carries with it all sorts of memories and emotions that can completely change how we are feeling in that moment. This is why many of have a workout playlist. It's because that music can get us so amped!

That's the sort of knowledge that the author of Second Peter tells us to support and strengthen our faith with. It's a knowledge that transcends our minds and resides in our hearts, affecting us on a basic and personal level.

Jesus' Knowledge of God

There is a period in Jesus' life that shows us what this virtue looks like in practice and why it's so vital to moving forward in life. In Matthew 3 we find Jesus being baptized by his cousin John:

13At that time Jesus came from Galilee to the Jordan River so that John would baptize him. 14John tried to stop him and said, "I need to be baptized by you, yet you come to me?"

15Jesus answered, "Allow me to be baptized now. This is necessary to fulfill all righteousness."

So John agreed to baptize Jesus. [16]When Jesus was baptized, he immediately came up out of the water. Heaven was opened to him, and he saw the Spirit of God coming down like a dove and resting on him. [17]A voice from heaven said, "This is my Son whom I dearly love; I find happiness in him." (Matthew 3:13-17)

This is really when Jesus' public ministry begins. Up to this point he really hasn't done anything that would be considered remarkable. He hasn't performed any miracles or given any great teachings. Yet when he comes up out of the water, the heavens are torn open and a voice is heard saying, "This is my Son whom I dearly love; I find happiness in him" (Matthew 3:17). So here, at the very beginning, before Jesus has done any of the extraordinary things that get written down, we see him receiving from God a blessing.

This is the God that Jesus reveals to us: the God who is a loving Father, whose first word to us is blessing, whose love and acceptance is undeserved. It isn't earned or achieved; it is simply given and received.

This was always something that was hard for me to grasp until I became a dad myself. I have three kids, and I've I loved them even before they were born. My wife and I decided that we would keep a separate journal for each kid, which we would start writing in as soon as we learned from the ultrasound who they were. My son Rowan is our oldest, and I'll never forget writing in his journal for the first time. I was blown away by the amount of love I had for him and I hadn't even met him yet. He hadn't even taken his first breath, and I was already crazy about him. My kids didn't have to do anything to deserve my love. It's always somehow been theirs. That's the only relationship in my life that works like that. Even with my wife, who I am crazy about, our love for one another wasn't always there, but it grew out of a relationship, a commitment. My love for my wife developed, but with my kids the love has always just been there. I love them because I'm their dad; that's just how it is. Now many of us have been hurt by our parents, and in our mind if God is anything like them we don't want anything to do with God. However, even if you had horrible parents, I can imagine that you still have an idea of what a great parent should be like. God is where the idea of a good parent comes from, and God's love for us is undeserved.

As incredible as love of God sounds, the question is, how deeply do we know it? Do we know it enough to trust it? Do we know it as information that takes up space in our heads, or has this knowledge made its way to our hearts?

What happens next in Jesus' life shows where his kr
God's love resides. Right after Jesus is baptized, he is le
wilderness to be tempted by the devil.

¹Then the Spirit led Jesus up into the wilderness so that the de
might tempt him. ²After Jesus had fasted for forty days and forty
nights, he was starving. ³The tempter came to him and said,
"Since you are God's Son, command these stones to become
bread."

⁴Jesus replied, "It's written, *People won't live only by bread, but
by every word spoken by God.*"

⁵After that the devil brought him into the holy city and stood
him at the highest point of the temple. He said to him, ⁶"Since
you are God's Son, throw yourself down; for it is written, *I will
command my angels concerning you, and they will take you up
in their hands so that you won't hit your foot on a stone.*"

⁷Jesus replied, "Again it's written, *Don't test the Lord your God.*"

⁸Then the devil brought him to a very high mountain and showed
him all the kingdoms of the world and their glory. ⁹He said, "I'll
give you all these if you bow down and worship me."

¹⁰Jesus responded, "Go away, Satan, because it's written, *You
will worship the Lord your God and serve only him.*" ¹¹The devil
left him, and angels came and took care of him.

(Matthew 4:1-11)

There is something important about the first two temptations
that I had never noticed until a friend pointed it out to me. The first
two temptations begin with the devil saying to Jesus, "Since you are
God's Son…" or, in another translation, "If you are the Son of God…"
(NRSV). Wait a minute. What did God just tell Jesus a few verses
earlier, when he was baptized? A voice from heaven told him that he
was in fact the Son of God.

That's always a temptation, isn't it? To doubt that we are loved and
accepted, to doubt that what God has said is true.

Jesus knew he was God's Son—truly knew it in his heart, not
only in his head. He responded to the devil's temptations with the
confidence and authority of one who knows his relationship to God
and rests secure within it. Because he knew it, trusted it, he did not
need to do anything to prove it.

...many of us know a lot of information about the ...ion is, has any of it made its way to our hearts? ...how that God loves unconditionally, and yet ...trying to earn that love and approval. We ...to never leave us or forsake us, and yet ...king risks. We may talk about the hope ...ur knowledge of God, but we continually find ...anxiety and despair. We know God as someone ...orgive, and yet we can't seem to forgive ourselves or ...around us. We know that the God we worship is recklessly ...us, and yet we hoard our time, our money, and our energy. We ...ay we know a God of abundant goodness, and yet we find ourselves stricken with envy and resentment when something good happens to someone else.

It's one thing for the truth of the gospel to be information that we know in our heads—it's quite another for us to truly take it in—to know it in the depths of our hearts.

When God told Jesus that he was loved and accepted, Jesus believed it and came to know it. And do you know how Jesus combated the devil's lies? With the Scriptures—with the truth of what God had said.

Spiritual Discipline

What we see from Jesus is an unwavering trust in who he was and how God felt about him. I don't believe that this sort of posture was automatic for Jesus. Hebrews 5:8 tells us that Jesus "learned obedience." I believe that his trust in what God had said was the result of rhythms and disciplines that were a part of his daily life, so that he came to know God's word as something that was ingrained deep within him.

Scripture tells us that from the time he was a little boy Jesus was a student of the word. In Luke 2, at the age of twelve, Jesus surprised the scholars at the Temple in Jerusalem with his understanding of the Scriptures (Luke 2:41-52). Before his confrontation with the devil in the wilderness, Jesus spent forty days and nights in prayer and fasting. Several times in the Gospels we are told how Jesus would withdraw to pray by himself, reconnecting with God.

We see in Jesus' example the importance of regularly reading and studying Scripture, of praying, of fasting. This is how we grow in knowledge—through these regular disciplines of learning, [ ] self-denial. This is how we add or supplement our faith and with knowledge.

Tell me, if Jesus himself had to practice these discipline to stay grounded in the truth, who are we to think that we c.... nave to? Our tendency is to want what Jesus has, but without being willing to do what it takes to have it. Supplementing our faith with knowledge is a matter of deepening our understanding and confidence of our new identity in Christ and making the truth of the gospel real in our lives through the practice of rhythms and disciplines like Scripture reading, prayer, and fasting.

A friend of mine shared with me once about how these disciplines and rhythms have impacted his life. He and his father have always had a really volatile relationship. Several years ago, all of their dysfunction came exploding to the surface in the form of a nasty fight. It didn't get physical, but my friend said he could remember feeling so much anger and resentment toward his dad, and it was obvious that his dad had many of the same feelings toward him. The blowup didn't resolve in any way, but instead it sort of blew over and they just acted like it never happened.

Well, after that incident my friend began to make some serious changes in his life. One of those changes was to commit to a regular practice of a few spiritual disciplines, such as prayer and Scripture reading, in a deeper way than he had before. He had grown up in the church his whole life, but to him the gospel was just information—it was all head knowledge that hadn't really made its way into his heart. Over the course of about a year, these disciplines became a part of my friend's everyday life as he committed himself to practicing them. They really began to make an impact on how he lived.

The impact of these disciplines became evident to him about a year after the big fight with his dad, when they got into another one. He said it was so strange. They were standing in the same room, he was looking at the same man, and they were arguing over the same issues; but when things started to get heated—when they started to get really ugly—he didn't respond in the same way that he had a year earlier. Before, when his dad got loud, he got loud. When his dad got angry, he got angry. But this time, he said that when he looked at his dad, anger wasn't the dominating emotion—what he felt more than anything was compassion. My friend told me that he looked at his father through all of his own frustration, and he was somehow able to see him as someone who was dealing with a lot of pain and brokenness himself. Where the first fight ended in them just continuing to ignore everything, this fight ended in them actually beginning to talk through some of their issues. It was almost the same exact situation, but two totally different responses. The only thing my friend could think of to explain his different reaction were these disciplines—the fact that this love of God was more of a reality in his life that it had been before.

Jesus says to us in John 15:4-5, "Remain in me, and I will remain in you. A branch can't produce fruit by itself, but must remain in the vine. Likewise, you can't produce fruit unless you remain in me. I am the vine; you are the branches. If you remain in me and I in you, then you will produce much fruit. Without me, you can't do anything." What word shows up over and over again in those verses? *Remain.* The word can also be translated as "abide," "dwell," or "make your home in." This is what growing in knowledge is all about. It's about remaining in Jesus—grounding ourselves in what is true and making it real in our lives through the practice of rhythms and disciplines.

So what are these disciplines? They include regular Scripture reading and study; prayer; fasting; meditation; worship; service; confession; silence. There are others as well, but this is a good list to give you some ideas of what spiritual disciplines might look like in your life. I don't have the space needed in this book to discuss, with any sort of depth, the various disciplines that followers of Jesus have been using for the past two thousand years. I would much rather point you to authors like Dallas Willard, author of *The Spirit of the Disciplines: Understanding How God Changes Lives* (HarperCollins, 1988), or Richard J. Foster, author of *Celebration of Discipline: The Path to Spiritual Growth* (HarperSanFrancisco, 1978). What I'm really interested in doing is to ask you this:

What does a commitment to growth in knowledge look like for you right now? Are you committed to any intentional and consistent practices? How much time and space are you carving out to point your soul at the things that matter most?

If you are reading this as a group, this is one of the ways you can push one another forward. Perhaps you want to commit to reading Scripture daily, or praying at certain times of the day. Maybe you attend worship sporadically, and you want to commit to attending every week moving forward. Or maybe you can take an intentional sabbath, truly resting one day per week. Or perhaps you will want to spend twenty minutes per day in silence, opening yourself to God's presence. Identify some disciplines that you can commit to, and create a rhythm for your life that will allow you to add knowledge to your faith and goodness. And then, in your small group, help one another stay faithful to these disciplines.

Learning and Fascination

It's important that we remember what these disciplines are for. They are for growing in knowledge and for seating that knowledge firmly within our hearts. They are for moving us forward. We don't need to approach them as rote exercises, but as gifts and tools to enable us to go deeper into the mystery of God.

Jesus' invitation to each of us is to be a *disciple*. That word means student. A disciple is one whose fundamental posture is that of a learner—someone who is constantly on the lookout for opportunities to grow, to discover something new, or perhaps to rediscover something he or she has forgotten.

Proverbs 9:10 says, "The beginning of wisdom is the fear of the LORD; / the knowledge of the holy one is understanding." This idea of the "fear of the Lord" is something that shows up over and over in the Proverbs. It isn't referring to paranoia about God, as if we have to live in constant anxiety because God is going to smite us at any time. (*Smite* . . . what a funny little word.) Fear of the Lord is referring to a sense of reverence toward a God who is bigger and more than we can possibly imagine. Fear of the Lord comes from a humble realization that we never gain any ground on God—that God is so far beyond us that there is always something new to learn about who God is and what God is like. Fear of the Lord is less about being afraid and more about being fascinated.

That is the attitude of a disciple—of a learner—it is a spirit of fascination.

Last January I decided to get myself back into shape. When my wife and I first started dating, I was a personal trainer and so my physical fitness was a big priority. Three kids later and, well, let's just say it has become much less of a priority. So last January I started running again. Our family had just moved into a neighborhood that is right next to an old golf course, which is no longer in operation. There are no sidewalks along any of the roads, so I decided to start running the abandoned golf cart paths that circled around our neighborhood. The paths were challenging because of all of the hills, but I was disappointed when I finished running them because they didn't add up to much. When I finished running them for the first time, my GPS told me that I had run only a little over a quarter of a mile. I was pretty bummed. It had certainly felt like way more than a quarter mile—those hills were brutal. And I realized that if I were going to get in a decent run, I would have to run the same loop over and over again. In fact, I can remember one Saturday morning running that thing twelve times in order to get three miles in. Twelve times!

After a couple of months of running, I knew everything about that course. I knew where the hills were, where the straightaways were, where that annoying dog lived who would come barking out of nowhere every single time. It was so boring!

A couple of months into this, a friend came to stay with us for a while. This guy was an actual runner. See, I'm just a guy who runs. There's a difference. Runners actually enjoy the act of running. People who run—like me—we don't like any of it. It's awful. Every single bit of it. (I got talked into running a 10k race with some friends a while back. They told me that I would love it—that when you run with all of those people, you get so caught up in it that you actually forget that you're running. They lied. Never once did I forget that I was running. I was painfully aware of it the whole time.) Anyway, my friend the runner asked me about the cart paths. I told him that hills make it challenging, but it's really short and so it can get old fast, especially when you run as far as he was planning. He decided he would start there and see how it went.

After my friend had been gone for over an hour, I started to get a little worried. Had the annoying dog somehow gotten hold of him? Surely he hadn't been running the same quarter of a mile for an hour, right?

Eventually he finally got back to the house, and I asked him how it went. He said he loved it. I was a little surprised, so I asked him if he had been running the same loop the whole time. "No, no, no," he said. "Have you ever looked across the street?"

"Looked across the street?" I replied.

"Yeah, you know how the cart path seems to dead-end at the bottom of the hill when you get to the road? Well, it doesn't actually stop there. If you look across the street, you can see that it keeps on going. In fact, I was able to run well over three miles before I had to repeat anything. It's actually a really beautiful run."

I had been running the same boring loop over and over again, when all the time there were miles—MILES—of new path that I had missed because I had never taken the time to look across the street.

I wonder if, for many of us, this is a picture of how v
lives. We have our routines—our default ways of thinkin
ways of doing things. We run the same loop every day wi.
new and nothing different. If we were to be honest with ourse.
we'd realize that we are bored. Our faith is stale. God seems distant,
and we haven't experienced any sort of growth in a while. We are still
struggling with the same issues and looking at the same maturity gap.
Yet all the while, there are new paths waiting for us—new things to
learn, new experiences to be had, new perspectives and insights to be
gained, new ways of looking at things. We will miss all these beautiful
things because we won't take the time to look across the street.

But if we do begin to explore, taking up some disciplines to keep
us moving, we will find ourselves going deeper and deeper into the
mystery of God. We will find our knowledge of God growing, not just
because we learn new facts but because these things become written
on the inner core of who we are.

There is a question I try to ask myself every single day: "What am
I learning?" It's my way of being sure to look across the street. The
habit of asking it on a daily basis wakes me up to the reality that each
day holds countless opportunities to learn something new—to grow
in my knowledge of what matters most—and to ground myself in the
truth of what God has made available to us in Jesus Christ.

It's one thing to hear a bit of good news. It's another thing to actually
trust it, to drink it in and allow it change you. Living a life of forward
movement, closing our maturity gap, is going to require us to add
knowledge to our faith and goodness. We'll come to know the gospel
in a way that moves beyond head knowledge and instead allows it to
make its home in our hearts. There are opportunities all around for us
to do just that if we will develop a habit of looking across the street.

In Your Group

Study Matthew 4:1-11

Read Matthew 4:1-11 on the following page and make note of the role that knowledge plays in Jesus' temptations. Consider the following questions as you read it, and answer them in the space provided:

1. What do you want to know more about?
2. What role does knowledge play in Jesus' response to temptation?
3. What sort of knowledge does Jesus exhibit? Knowledge of what or of whom?
4. What about this passage encourages you or challenges you?
5. How would you describe, in one sentence, what this passage teaches us about knowledge?

Matthew 4:1-11

¹Then the Spirit led Jesus up into the wilderness so that the devil might tempt him. ²After Jesus had fasted for forty days and forty nights, he was starving. ³The tempter came to him and said, "Since you are God's Son, command these stones to become bread."

⁴Jesus replied, "It's written, *People won't live only by bread, but by every word spoken by God."*

⁵After that the devil brought him into the holy city and stood him at the highest point of the temple. He said to him, ⁶"Since you are God's Son, throw yourself down; for it is written, *I will command my angels concerning you, and they will take you up in their hands so that you won't hit your foot on a stone."*

⁷Jesus replied, "Again it's written, *Don't test the Lord your God."*

⁸Then the devil brought him to a very high mountain and showed him all the kingdoms of the world and their glory. ⁹He said, "I'll give you all these if you bow down and worship me."

¹⁰Jesus responded, "Go away, Satan, because it's written, *You will worship the Lord your God and serve only him."* ¹¹The devil left him, and angels came and took care of him.

What Resonates With You?

What from this session resonated with you? How did the reflection on knowledge encourage you or inspire you, and how did it challenge you? Remember from session 1 that it's important to pay attention to both—how we are encouraged and how we are challenged!

What encouraged you?

What challenged you?

Knowledge

What is the difference between head knowledge and heart knowledge? In the space below, make a list of the things you know in your heart, the way you know your favorite song. What significant spiritual truths do you know on this deep level?

What role does knowledge play in dealing with your maturity gap? In the space below, describe the distance between your ideal and your real with respect to knowledge or spiritual understanding. (You may find it helpful to draw a picture as well as write.) What steps can you take to close this gap?

Spiritual Disciplines

Are you currently committed to any sort of intentional disciplines or practices? If so, in the space below make a list of the ones you practice and include the frequency and intensity with which you do them. Then describe how they have strengthened your faith and deepened your knowledge. If not, share which spiritual disciplines sound most promising for you. What about them feels appealing? What do you hope to gain from adopting one of them?

Make a list of your key spiritual practices and how they lead to knowledge and strengthen faith.

What is the relationship between knowledge and spiritual discipline in your life? How do regular disciplines shape what we know, or add to it? How do they move what we know from our heads only down into our hearts?

Forward Goals

How can you and your fellow group members push one another forward when it comes to growing in knowledge? Remember: Try to set practical goals that can be accomplished and that you can hold each other accountable to. Discuss also how you will hold one another accountable.

What goals will help you move toward greater knowledge?

Session 3
Self-Control

This session is going to require you to use all of your senses. Before you go any further, I want you to go and find a piece of chocolate. It doesn't matter what kind, just a small piece of chocolate like a Hershey's Kiss or something like that. I'm serious. Go get one. Now!

If you don't like chocolate, then I want you to phone a friend and have them pray for you. That's just not right. OK, I'm kidding. Mostly. If you don't like chocolate, then go get your favorite tasty treat. But to keep things simple, I'm going to write as if everyone has some chocolate.

Once you have the chocolate, here's what I want you to do: If it's in a wrapper, go ahead and open it up, but don't eat it! Just take a look at that beautiful piece of black gold. Notice its texture, how smooth it is. That looks good doesn't it?

Now I want you to smell it. Mmm, smells good, doesn't it? Is it making your mouth water? Don't eat it! Here's what I want you to do next: Put it down right next to you, and let's have a conversation about... self-control.

We have been working our way through a fascinating passage in 2 Peter 1:3-11. Verses 5-7 of that passage present us with a picture of what it looks like to grow in maturity—that is, completeness or wholeness. It's a picture of what it looks like to move forward in life toward who we have the power to be in Christ.

God is often made to seem like some cosmic Debbie Downer who just wants to rain on our parade, who loves to point out all of the ways in which we have it wrong and to keep us from having any fun. For many people, following Jesus has been made to seem like a miserable existence that requires us to deny our humanity and abstain from all of the things that we truly enjoy in life. But this couldn't be further from the truth. In fact, it's sort of funny—Jesus was often criticized for having too much fun! The way of Jesus isn't about denying our humanity; instead it's an invitation to discover what true humanity really is. Remember: Jesus not only shows us who God is, he also reveals to us who we were meant to be. He reveals the version of humanity that God is ultimately making us into.

Right in the middle of this passage in Second Peter, the author lists seven virtues, undergirded by faith, that point us forward toward a full, restored humanity. The first two are moral excellence (goodness) and knowledge. And the third virtue in our list is self-control.

Who wouldn't benefit from some more self-control? Am I right? In fact, how's that chocolate doing down there? If you've already folded and eaten it, go and get another piece. But don't eat it this time!

I can imagine that we all would love to see some more self-control in our lives. Yet once again, we are confronted with what we have been calling our maturity gap: the distance between our ideal self and our real self—the gap between who we want to be, or who we know we could be, and who we presently are. As frustrating as this gap is, self-control is at the center of what it's going to take to begin to close it. In a way, self-control is the muscle that puts to work everything we have talked about so far—faith, goodness, and knowledge all get put to use and developed through the practice of self-control.

Self-Governance

We often have a narrow understanding of *self-control*. When we hear that word, we tend to think of it only in terms of resistance or abstinence. Self-control is all about saying no to things. The biblical idea of self-control is a bit more complex than that. The word Greek word used here in Second Peter, *egkrateia*, is related to words meaning might, power, mastery, or dominion. So this word might also be translated as something like "self-mastery" or "self-governance." In this understanding, a person of self-control isn't someone who just says no, but a person who is able to govern himself or herself. It's a person who masters and directs his or her appetites and desires in way that is healthy. Biblical self-control speaks to a wide-ranging self-mastery that goes beyond just resistance or abstinence.

Scripture teaches that you and I are integrated beings. We are both physical and spiritual creatures. Being a physical creature means having a body, which also means having natural appetites and desires. When you hear that word *appetite*, what do you immediately think of? Food. That's because you have a physical appetite for food. It's so natural that I bet I could just mention a certain restaurant and make you hungry.

Chipotle.

Some of you may no longer be able to pay attention to me, because you will be mentally swimming in cilantro lime rice. I understand.

Anyway, as physical beings we have all sorts of different appetites. The appetite for food is the one we think of right away, but there are others. Of course, there's the appetite for sex—for intimacy. We also have an appetite for connection and companionship, which is why the right people can make just about any situation a good time. We have an appetite for significance, in that we all want to matter and make a contribution. We have an appetite for success—we love to accomplish things, whether it's getting ahead at work or even organizing our sock drawer. We have an appetite for adventure, or to experience new things, which is why we love to buy new things, go to new places, or simply watch a new movie.

These appetites are a part of our physical nature, and they are innate in all of us. These desires are incredibly strong, too. They can pull us in all sorts of different directions, and they can be powerful motivators. If you're still thinking about Chipotle, you know exactly what I mean.

What we have to understand is that our desires, our appetites are not bad in and of themselves. In fact, they are God-given. However, these appetites, which are a part of our physical nature, are meant to be guided and directed by the spirit.

We can get a little creeped out by that word *spirit*, but we really don't need to be. Our spiritual nature is that place where our hopes and dreams come from. It's that place where we long for meaning and purpose; it's that place where our "why" questions come from. We are spiritual creatures. That's why we can satisfy some of these appetites and enjoy them more deeply than just in a physical way. Some things also impact us spiritually. Certain movies are not only fun to watch, but we walk away from them thinking about our own lives in different ways. Or a great conversation with a close friend can actually empower us, making us feel stronger. Or in a Communion meal of bread and wine, things that normally satisfy physical appetites take on powerful spiritual significance.

We are physical and spiritual beings; and although these two natures are different, they are not separate. They are integrated; they are meant to exist together and in a particular order. I love the picture we are given in Genesis 2:7 of how God created human beings. It says that "the Lord God formed the human from the topsoil of the fertile land and blew life's breath into his nostrils. The human came to life." It is the spiritual aspect—the breath of God—that animates and gives life, meaning, and purpose to the physical. The philosopher Dallas Willard says, "Spirituality is simply the holistic quality of human life as it was meant to be, at the center of which is our relation to God."[1] It is our spirit, namely that which connects us to God, that is meant to guide and direct our natural desires and our physical lives.

Where we get into trouble is when that order gets messed up and when our appetites start calling the shots. This can be incredibly destructive, and it is exactly why we have this maturity gap—why there is this distance between our ideal and our real. One way to understand self-control is that it's about restoring the proper order in our lives, realigning our physical and spiritual lives in a way that reflects our relation to God. The big question then is, "How do we do that?" The author of Second Peter doesn't leave us hanging. He writes a few important things at the beginning of our passage that I believe will help us discover how we can have more self-control in our lives.

The Enemy of Self-Control

I said earlier that self-control isn't just a matter of resistance or restraint, but it most certainly starts there. The last part of verse 4 speaks of escaping "from the world's immorality that sinful craving produces." Sinful craving is another way of talking about harmful desires, or lust.

Lust is the enemy of self-control.

That word *lust* is often associated with sexual desire, and that is part of it. But lust, or "sinful craving" as the author of Second Peter speaks of it, is also far larger than that. It's not just sexual desire. Sinful craving refers to any situation where the physical and spiritual order gets messed up. Or as another way to understand it, lust is any time we look to a physical or natural appetite to fulfill a deeper spiritual need.

Remember our spiritual nature is our relation to God. We were created to find our worth, our value, our identity, our "why," from our connection to God. Lust is whenever we look to one of our natural appetites to do that for us instead. It's not hard to recognize how this shows up in our lives in all sorts of destructive ways.

When our appetite for food is elevated too highly, we will use food as a substitute for God, and the refrigerator becomes our place of worship. It's where we go for validation. Or our appetite to be known, if it isn't managed by our spiritual life, can lead to all sorts of unhealthy behavior. Some of us talk too much. We can absolutely dominate a conversation, and most of the time we aren't really listening to what other people say. We are just waiting for our turn to talk. This comes from this unmanaged appetite to be known, to be heard, to be recognized. Or our appetite for significance, if it goes unmanaged, will cause us to wrap our self-worth in how we measure up to the people around us. How people treat us will determine how we feel about ourselves. If our appetite for security gets elevated to an unhealthy place, it can lead to anxiety and worry. Our appetite for comfort can lead to laziness, or we get consumed in mindless hobbies like organizing our Pinterest account or managing our fantasy football team.

Lust is whenever we look to one of our natural appetites to satisfy a deeper spiritual need, and it is the enemy of self-control. The author of Second Peter has a word for us concerning lust, and it's *escape*. Escape! Run away! Lust is incredibly dangerous, and the author of Second Peter lifts up escape from it as a worthy goal.

For one thing, lust is deceptive. It's built on a lie. It promises way more than it can deliver. Have you ever noticed how after you indulge in a craving, there is typically a sort of letdown? Not long ago I bought the newest iPhone. I watched the commercials and saw my friend's new iPhone, and was convinced that I had to have it. After I bought it, I was thrilled. But about twelve hours later, I realized that my new phone was still . . . just a phone.

Lust is built on a lie. It tells us that this appetite can fulfill that deeper spiritual need for God, but in truth it can't. So when we do eat the whole box, when we do go to the computer screen, take the drink, exaggerate the truth, get our hands on the next new thing, it may satisfy for a moment but it doesn't last. And we are left feeling hungrier, emptier, lonelier than we were before.

This is exactly the lie that the serpent used with Adam and Eve in Genesis 3. He made them believe that God was withholding something from them, that there was something other than God that they were missing. We all know how that turned out. We've been buying into a similar lie ever sense.

Not only is lust deceptive, it's also destructive. Pursuing our cravings always costs us something. Lust entices us to give in to the immediate at the expense of the important. When one of our appetites gets inflamed, often what happens is that we get so fixated on satisfying it that we ignore everything else. Typically what we don't see is what giving in to lust is going to cost us.

We see this from a guy named Esau in the Book of Genesis. One day he comes home from the field, and he is so consumed with hunger that his brother, Jacob, convinces him to sell his birthright for a bowl of soup (Genesis 25:27-34). As the oldest son, Esau stood to inherit a sizable portion of his father's wealth as his birthright. Is any bowl of soup worth a fortune? When you ask the question like that it sounds ridiculous, but it's actually quite sad because things like it happen all the time.

A person in an affair gets so caught up in gratifying an out-of-control appetite that he or she loses sight of what it is actually going to cost. Is that "bowl of soup" really worth the potential lost respect of one's children and grandchildren? Is it worth deceit and alienation, hurt and heartache?

A shady business deal may make you some money, but what is the profit going to cost you? Or the false sense of intimacy one might get from a certain website may give a thrill in the moment, but it will cost a great deal in terms of true intimacy with one's spouse. And how many people have turned their backs on their loved ones and their future for the sake of an addiction?

Of course, that "bowl of soup" purchase happens in more subtle ways as well. For example, for my wife and me it has become so easy and even second-nature to pull out our phones whenever we get a moment to ourselves. We get a few spare seconds and mindlessly peruse our various social media accounts. I'm sure you've witnessed this scene before: A family is out to dinner and no one is talking to one another other because their heads are down and their faces are blue from the light of their phones. A lot of the time we aren't doing it because we are interested, but just because it has become a habit. And make no mistake, it is costing us. It's costing us in intimacy and connection with one another; it's costing us the ability to be fully present in the moment. We're trading limited, priceless moments with those we love to read a status update that we'll forget in thirty seconds.

It makes no sense and yet it happens all the time. We sell it all for a bowl of soup.

The author of Second Peter tells us to escape, flee, run away from cravings that will consume us. Perhaps what we need more than anything is a wake-up call. Chances are if you're human, there's some sort of lust, some sort of destructive pattern or bad habit that you think you have control of, and the truth is you don't. Make no mistake: If it continues, it will cost you something.

The Power of Confession

One of the biggest reasons why you and I continue to struggle with the same destructive things is because, well, we just want to. We aren't totally willing to remove certain temptations from our lives. Whether it's another person, a place, a substance, or a possession, we allow them to remain because we still want there to be an opportunity for us to give in to them. If we want to experience maturity, completeness—if we want to close the gap between our ideal and our real and move forward—then we are going to have to do whatever it takes to remove that unhealthy thing from our lives.

This almost always begins with confession, and I'm not just talking about between you and God, but between you and another person. James 5:16 says, "Confess your sins to each other and pray for each other so that you may be healed." Confessing our sins *to each other* brings them into the light, and it makes possible prayer and support in being healed from them. As long as they stay hidden, they will more than likely show back up. But getting them out into the open is the first step in breaking their control over us.

There is a scene at the end of the movie *8 Mile* that illustrates the power of confession. The movie *8 Mile* came out in 2002 and stars Eminem, who plays the part of Jimmy, also known as Rabbit. Jimmy is a blue-collar factory worker who comes from a poor family, who has just recently moved back home with his alcoholic mother. Jimmy is also an aspiring rapper, and he enters into a rap battle competition. He eventually finds himself in the championship match with his nemesis, Papa Doc, who has humiliated Jimmy in the past. The point of a rap battle is to humiliate your opponent by calling out all of his or her flaws and weaknesses. When it comes time for the final match, Jimmy finds out that he has to go first, which is usually a disadvantage. Jimmy, however, turns it into an advantage. Instead of rapping about his opponent, he raps about himself. He says all of the things that he knows Papa Doc is going to say, and in doing so he takes away all of his ammunition. I love his last line. Before handing over the mic, Jimmy says to Papa Doc, "Here, tell these people something they don't know about me."

That my friends, is the power of confession. It is the first step to gaining self-control. When we own our junk, our junk stops owning us.

Speaking of owning our junk, let's take a little "chocolate break." Go ahead and pick it up and give it a good smell. Still smell good? Don't eat it! Just make sure it's still there looking all yummy. Once again, if you have already eaten it, go and get another one, but try to hold on to this one until the end.

From Resistance to Redirection

Self-control begins with resistance, but it doesn't stop there. According to the author of Second Peter, God's divine power has given us everything we need. For what? For helping just say no to things? Well, no...God's divine power has given us everything we need *to live a godly life*. God's promises enable us to do more than just resist all of the stuff that controls us; they empower us to participate in the divine nature (2 Peter 1:3). If we keep God's power and promises in mind, we can see that self-control isn't just a matter of resistance, but also a matter of redirection. It isn't only a matter of saying no to what enslaves us. It's also a matter of saying yes to what fully gives us life.

In Luke 11, Jesus likens us to a house and says, "When an impure spirit comes out of a person it goes through arid places seeking rest and does not find it. Then it says, 'I will return to the house I left.' When it arrives, it finds the house swept clean and put in order. Then it goes and takes seven other spirits more wicked than itself, and they go in and live there. And the final condition of that person is worse than the first" (Luke 11:24-26 NIV). The house doesn't just need to be swept clean. The house needs a new resident—a new Lord. Resisting or removing a negative force is only half the challenge. Remember, self-control is a matter of self-governance, the ability to direct and guide our inner selves in a way that is healthy. Self-control sets us free to make ourselves fully available to that which brings us life.

A fascinating passage in Ephesians sums up this idea well, as Paul talks about the need for Christians to put aside an old way of life in order adopt new life in Christ:

17So I'm telling you this, and I insist on it in the Lord: you shouldn't live your life like the Gentiles anymore. They base their lives on pointless thinking, 18and they are in the dark in their reasoning. They are disconnected from God's life because of their ignorance and their closed hearts. 19They are people who lack all sense of right and wrong, and who have turned themselves over to doing whatever feels good and to practicing every sort of corruption along with greed.

20But you didn't learn that sort of thing from Christ. 21Since you really listened to him and you were taught how the truth is in Jesus, 22change the former way of life that was part of the person you once were, corrupted by deceitful desires. 23Instead, renew the thinking in your mind by the Spirit 24and clothe yourself with the new person created according to God's image in justice and true holiness.

25Therefore, after you have gotten rid of lying, *Each of you must tell the truth to your neighbor* because we are parts of each other in the same body. 26*Be angry without sinning.* Don't let the sun set on your anger. 27Don't provide an opportunity for the devil. 28Thieves should no longer steal. Instead, they should go to work, using their hands to do good so that they will have something to share with whoever is in need.

29Don't let any foul words come out of your mouth. Only say what is helpful when it is needed for building up the community so that it benefits those who hear what you say. 30Don't make the Holy Spirit of God unhappy—you were sealed by him for the day of redemption. 31Put aside all bitterness, losing your temper, anger, shouting, and slander, along with every other evil. 32Be kind, compassionate, and forgiving to each other, in the same way God forgave you in Christ.

(Ephesians 4:17-32)

In verses 22-24, Paul says, "...change the former way of life that was part of the person you once were, corrupted by deceitful desires. Instead, renew the thinking in your mind by the Spirit and clothe yourself with the new person created according to God's image in justice and true holiness." In Paul's view, Jesus call's us away from our old life and invites us into a new one. There is a movement from resistance to redirection—to put off what we once were and to put on what is now offered to us in Jesus. We put away the old self so that we might put on the new. Self-control is our recurring decision to keep choosing the new self.

Paul then goes on to give us some practical examples of how this might play out in our lives. In verse 28 he says to us, "Thieves should no longer steal." Pretty straightforward, right? Don't steal. It begins with resistance, but it doesn't stop there. Paul goes on to say, "Instead, they should go to work, using their hands to do good so that they will have something to share with whoever is in need." Do you see the movement from resistance to redirection? Later, in verse 29 he says, "Don't let any foul words come out of your mouth" (resistance), but instead, "Only say what is helpful when it is needed for building up the community so that it benefits those who hear what you say" (redirection).

Resistance by itself doesn't work; it doesn't fully constitute self-control. When we are told not to do something, how often are we truly compelled not to do it, especially if it's something we really enjoy? If all of our energy and attention is on what we shouldn't do, then we are still focused on what we shouldn't do. The real question is, how can we redirect our energy toward something that is good and healthy?

This is why so many of us struggle with self-control. We are good at identifying what we need to say "no" to, but we rarely take the next step in identifying what we ought to be saying "yes" to.

Don't just try to resist an affair. Redirect—invest in your marriage.

Don't just say no to certain foods. Redirect—learn to pursue health in every aspect of your life.

Don't just try to say less. Redirect—try to listen more.

Don't just try to be less busy. Redirect—strive to be more intentional and more fruitful by carving out time for the stuff that actually matters.

Our appetites themselves aren't bad; they are God-given. But they can become destructive when they are pointed in the wrong direction. Self-control is about doing the hard work of identifying what is the good thing behind the lust, the bad habit, the destructive pattern. Self-control is about how we can harness it and point it in the right direction, in a way that draws us closer to God and allows us to close our maturity gap and move forward.

And here's the thing: You can do this. You. Can. Do. This. How do I know? Well consider how the passage in Second Peter begins: God's power has given us everything we need to live a godly life. Self-control is a fruit of the Spirit. It is something we have because God's power has given it to us.

Elsewhere in Scripture, we read that the same spirit that raised Christ from the dead is the spirit that is at work in us (Romans 8:11). Now that is some power. When we said yes to Jesus, the same life-giving power that defeated death itself was unleashed in you and in me. What if we lived with an awareness of that power? What if, every time we were tempted to give in to that lust, to compromise, to settle for less, we stopped ourselves and said, "I don't have to do this"?

Why don't you go ahead and pick up that chocolate. Here's what I want you to: Eat it, pay attention to how good it tastes. First Timothy 4:4 says, "For everything God created is good, and nothing is to be rejected if it is received with thanksgiving" (NIV). Pay attention to the details and thank God for every single one of them, because that is essentially what self-control is about. It isn't about denying ourselves what it means to be a human being or denying ourselves of all the pleasures of life. It's about enjoying those things for what they truly are—not artificial replacements for God, but good gifts from God—gifts to be managed, to be embraced, to be enjoyed. Here's to tasting just how good life is.

In Your Group

Study Ephesians 4:17-32

Read Ephesians 4:17-32 on the following page and make note of the role self-control plays in the author's view of our new life in Christ. Consider the following questions as you read it, and answer them in the space provided:

1. What do you want to know more about?
2. Why does the author of this passage encourage self-control?
3. Where in this passage do you see a movement from resistance to redirection?
4. What about this passage encourages you or challenges you?
5. How would you describe what this passage teaches about self-control? How would you describe the relationship between self-control, knowledge, and faith?

Ephesians 4:17-32

¹⁷So I'm telling you this, and I insist on it in the Lord: you shouldn't live your life like the Gentiles anymore. They base their lives on pointless thinking, ¹⁸and they are in the dark in their reasoning. They are disconnected from God's life because of their ignorance and their closed hearts. ¹⁹They are people who lack all sense of right and wrong, and who have turned themselves over to doing whatever feels good and to practicing every sort of corruption along with greed.

²⁰But you didn't learn that sort of thing from Christ. ²¹Since you really listened to him and you were taught how the truth is in Jesus, ²²change the former way of life that was part of the person you once were, corrupted by deceitful desires. ²³Instead, renew the thinking in your mind by the Spirit ²⁴and clothe yourself with the new person created according to God's image in justice and true holiness.

²⁵Therefore, after you have gotten rid of lying, *Each of you must tell the truth to your neighbor* because we are parts of each other in the same body. ²⁶*Be angry without sinning.* Don't let the sun set on your anger. ²⁷Don't provide an opportunity for the devil. ²⁸Thieves should no longer steal. Instead, they should go to work, using their hands to do good so that they will have something to share with whoever is in need.

²⁹Don't let any foul words come out of your mouth. Only say what is helpful when it is needed for building up the community so that it benefits those who hear what you say. ³⁰Don't make the Holy Spirit of God unhappy—you were sealed by him for the day of redemption. ³¹Put aside all bitterness, losing your temper, anger, shouting, and slander, along with every other evil. ³²Be kind, compassionate, and forgiving to each other, in the same way God forgave you in Christ.

What Resonates With You?

What from this session resonates with you? How did the message about self-control encourage you, and how did it challenge you? Keep in mind the benefits that can come from recognizing when we are challenged, as well as when we are inspired!

What encouraged you?

What challenged you?

Self-Governance

How does it change your understanding of self-control if you think of it as self-governance or self-mastery? Is it something more than just restraining oneself, and if so, what else does it involve? In the space below, describe the difference between self-restraint and self-control. Which one is easier to achieve?

The Enemy of Self-Control

What does lust mean based on the discussion above, and why is lust the enemy of self-control? In the space below, list examples of lust that you struggle with, keeping in mind that lust is not just sexual in nature. What would it look like for you to practice self-control in these areas?

What is the relationship between desires, or appetites, and self-control? How can the ideas of resistance and redirection allow for good desires and healthy ways to pursue them? Considering the "lusts" you identified in the previous question, identify which good desires lie beneath the out-of-control desires. What would redirection of these desires look like?

Forward Goals

How can you and your fellow group members push one another forward when it comes to helping one another grow in self-control? Be sure to think about these goals in terms of both resistance and redirection—not just identifying how you will show restraint, but how you will put your energy into other, better things instead. As before, identify goals that are specific and practical. And describe how you and your fellow group members will hold one another accountable.

What goals will help you move toward the virtue of self-control?

Session 4
Perseverance

I shared with you in an earlier session that for the past year, I have been working to get back in shape. I've wanted to make my physical health more of a priority. To help get me started, I decided to try something called Whole30. Essentially Whole30 is a thirty-day cleanse or fast that is supposed to help curb your cravings and rid your body of bad stuff. It involves totally avoiding added sugar, dairy, and processed foods, among other things—the bad stuff. Trouble is, I like the bad stuff. I mean I *really* like the bad stuff. The badder the better.

Whole30 is intense. I knew that it was going to be really hard for me to commit to it, and so I decided to make a calendar of sorts to guide me. I wrote the numbers one through thirty on a piece of paper, and then slapped it up on the fridge. My plan was to cross off each day that I was able to make it through without cheating. I figured that actually seeing my progress like this would help me generate some momentum. At first it did. I'll never forget how good it felt to cross off day number one. In fact, I crossed that number out in slow-motion while some epic music played in the background. My wife was so proud, my kids were cheering for me, and I was already thinking about buying my first pair of skinny jeans.

You probably know where this is headed, don't you? I think I made it about four days before I fell off the proverbial wagon. I didn't just fall off the wagon; I got run over by the wagon. It turns out that

Whole30 was a whole lot of nothing for me, at least the first time I tried it.

I have a feeling that you can relate to this. When it comes to making changes in our lives, moving forward, and closing our maturing gaps, we often have big ambitions and good intentions. But if you're anything like me, you combine these great intentions with poor follow-through.

Our New Year's celebrations are a great example of this, with those so-called resolutions we set every year. A better name for them would be something like our New Year *traditions*, because we tend to make the same ones very year, don't we? Then, usually around March, we start making those "adjustments" to the commitments we have made.

"Did I really say I was going to do that?"

"You know with my schedule, I just don't have the time."

"In this season of my life, or in the environment that I work in and the people I work with, that just isn't very realistic. I don't need to be so hard on myself."

Sound familiar?

We slip up, fudge, and make excuses until eventually we have conveniently forgotten about all of those goals, resolutions, or whatever we call them. That is, until the next year when we will make virtually the same ones.

Chances are you recognize this in yourself, because it's common for many of us. So if that is the case, how do we get any sort of sustained positive movement? How do we get forward momentum to stick around for very long? This is an important question, because at the heart of this study lies a commitment to moving forward, to progressing in our spiritual lives so that we become the kind of people God has empowered us to be.

Again and Again and Again

This brings us to the next virtue in our passage from Second Peter—endurance. The author exhorts us to add endurance to self-control (and to knowledge, moral excellence [goodness], and faith). Other translations use the word *perseverance* (NIV), which better captures the meaning of the Greek word as I'll explain below. Now in this list of virtues, the author is adapting an ancient literary form called the *sorites*. This was a popular form of instruction in the ancient world where a teacher would link together various virtues or vices, but not necessarily in a sequential order. So, the author of Second Peter believed all of these virtues are important and connected to one another. But he didn't necessarily believe we have to grow in these virtues in the particular order that they are listed.[1] However, I do think it is interesting that the virtue of endurance, or perseverance, comes right after self-control.

Anybody who has demonstrated any type of self-control knows that there are two conflicting emotional responses. At first, you feel this incredible high that comes from the victory you just had. You did it, you resisted the temptation or did the hard thing! But then that high is eventually followed by a powerful low: the sobering reality that you are going to have to practice self-control in that area again and again and again.

You finally wake up on time to make it to the 6:00 a.m. class over at the gym. After the workout, you feel great! You feel like you could conquer the world. You've got "Eye of the Tiger" playing on repeat in your head all day long. But then the alarm clock goes off the next morning, and you have to fight the same battle all over again. Where did "Eye of the Tiger" go?

This can be incredibly overwhelming. Often we don't realize how big our maturity gap is until we take a few steps toward our ideal and get a feel for how far we still have to go. When we recognize just how far the distance is, what typically happens is we quit. We convince ourselves that our real isn't all that bad, that maybe our ideal isn't so desirable after all. We give up believing that we can change, or that we need to change. And the scary thing is that when we relapse like this, we tend to fall back even further than we were before we had the victory.

What you and I need now on our journey forward, toward maturity, is the strength to put what God has given to us to work not just once, but again and again and again. This is what endurance or perseverance is all about.

First, let's make an effort to understand what this word actually means.

For me, the word *endurance* conjures up images of distance running. I told you already how I feel about running. I . . . don't enjoy it. Remember, I run but I'm not a runner.

The other translation, perseverance, at first seems even worse. It honestly sounds a little boring. It's often used as a synonym for patience. Yuck. Patience seems like such a weak and passive word. It doesn't exactly get us all fired up does it? Endurance might get some of us fired up (not me), but patience really doesn't do the trick.

But perseverance is more than patience. It's more active. Webster's dictionary defines perseverance as, "continued effort to do or achieve something despite difficulties, failure, or opposition."[2] That's actually pretty good. Effort. Achievement. Pushing through difficulties, failure, or opposition. It definitely sounds more exciting than patience.

I still think we can do better, though. The Greek word in Second Peter translated as endurance or perseverance is *hupomone*, which means something like courageous steadfastness. Here's my favorite definition of the word, from *The Exegetical Dictionary of the New Testament*: It "refers overwhelmingly—and positively—to independent, unyielding, defiant perseverance in the face of aggressive misfortune, and thus to a kind of courageousness."[3] There is nothing boring about that!

As a mental image, we might imagine Greek soldiers in battle standing strong and firm despite facing a much stronger force. If you have seen the movie *300*, think of Leonidas and his three hundred brave Spartan warriors, who held the pass of Thermopylae against the massive Persian army that vastly outnumbered them. That's hupomone, endurance or perseverance. It's apparently really good for your abs. (That last part is only funny if you have seen the movie.)

Perseverance isn't boring, and it most certainly isn't passive. It is this unyielding, defiant steadfastness in the face of powerful circumstances. And Second Peter mentions this virtue because it plays an important role in our forward journey toward maturity.

It's found in other Scripture passages, too. James 1:2-4 says, "My brothers and sisters, think of the various tests you encounter as occasions for joy. After all, you know that the testing of your faith produces endurance. Let this endurance complete its work so that you may be fully mature, complete, and lacking in nothing." There it is. Endurance is the hard work of maturity, of becoming whole and complete. The author of Second Peter has told us that we have been given nothing less than God's power and everything we need to live a godly life (2 Peter 1:3). Endurance, perseverance, is about putting that power to work.

Maturity isn't something that happens to us in an instant, but it is the result of what some have called, "long obedience in the same direction."[4]

The Hard Work

In his book *Outliers*, Malcolm Gladwell talks about what he refers to as the ten-thousand-hour rule. It's based on research and studies that have been done on the people who have achieved greatness in their craft, in an effort to understand what it is that sets them apart from everyone else. In whatever field, what is it that separates the truly great ones from the rest of the pack? The research Gladwell used found that the number one factor that separates these people from everyone else is the ten-thousand-hour rule. The ones who achieved greatness had spent somewhere around ten thousand hours, or about ten years' worth of really intense, hard practice, working on their craft. There were of course other factors involved like innate ability or talent, opportunities, and resources that were available to them. But the number one thing that separated the great ones from everyone else is that they worked harder than everyone else. They endured or persevered. They *hupomone*-ed. They kept showing up. In his book, Gladwell says, "The thing that distinguishes one performer from another is how hard he or she works. That's it. And what's more, the people at the very top don't work just harder or even much harder than everyone else. They work much, much harder."[5]

This may sound like common sense, but we have to park here for a moment. We must understand this and take it in. Because typically when it comes to our lack of maturity, to our lack of completeness, we can be so quick to blame everything else but our own lack of endurance.

It's because of how we were raised...
It's because of where we come from...
It's because of what that person did or didn't do...
It's because we can't seem to catch a break...
It's because of all the ways in which things didn't go our way...
It's because the doors keep getting shut in our face...

These are factors when it comes to our maturity gaps, but they certainly aren't excuses. At some point, we are going to have to face the hard truth that we all have a maturity gap and that it's within our power to close it. But that will take hard work, endurance. Some of us have inherited our maturity gaps, and some of ours are bigger than others' for reasons that aren't necessarily our fault. But every single person's maturity gap gets closed in the same way: through perseverance. We move forward by taking what God has made available to us in Jesus Christ, through the power of the Holy Spirit, and putting it to work.

I'm not suggesting that we can come to this place of maturity or wholeness by working hard purely on our own strength. That's not the gospel, and that isn't good news. Remember where all of this begins — with faith. All of these virtues are rooted within and grown from trust in the saving love of God that is made known to us with the cross and the empty tomb. We Protestants love to remind ourselves that we are saved through grace, and we should. It's all grace; it's all a free gift.

At the same time, we have to understand that grace is not opposed to hard work. It's not like once we say yes to Jesus, we just put it on cruise control and sit back and wait for God to fix us. Experiencing the reality of our salvation requires our participation, our cooperation with God. It requires endurance, taking the gift of the Holy Spirit and putting it to work. Paul says it so succinctly in Colossians 1:29 when he says, "I work hard and struggle for this goal with his energy, which works in me powerfully."

Our hard work. God's power.

This is what perseverance is all about. It's about putting the unbelievable resources that God has given us to work, relying upon God's power. Not just in the beginning. Not just once in a while. But on a day-by-day, moment-by-moment basis.

Shortsightedness

What might be helpful here is to spend some time digging into why we often don't do that. Let's look a little closer at why we struggle with perseverance. The author of Second Peter says something really interesting toward the end of the passage we've been exploring. In verse 8, after listing all of the virtues of maturity, the author goes on to say, "If all these are yours and they are growing in you, they'll keep you from becoming inactive and unfruitful in the knowledge of our Lord Jesus Christ" (2 Peter 1:8). In other words, if you persevere in these qualities, your experience with Jesus will not be for nothing. You will be active and fruitful. You can and will change.

Then the author goes on: "Whoever lacks these things is shortsighted and blind, forgetting that they were cleansed from their past sins" (2 Peter 1:9). So, the person who does not endure in cultivating these virtues is nearsighted to the point of being blind. Shortsightedness is the enemy of perseverance.

People who are shortsighted get so fixated on what is right in front of them — the internal struggle to do what is right or the external challenges they face—they get so fixated on those things that they lose sight of the big picture. They forget that their past sins have been cleansed. They relapse. Shortsightedness is the enemy of perseverance.

One of the author's main reasons for writing Second Peter is that some of the people in the church had allowed their shortsightedness to get the best of them. In the early church there was a general belief that the return of Christ would happen during the lifetime of the first generation of Christians. When that didn't happen, there were some who began to question whether it would ever happen. For instance, in chapter 3 we read "Most important, know this: in the last day scoffers will come, jeering, living by their own cravings, and saying 'Where is the promise of his coming? After all, nothing has changed—not since the beginning of creation, nor even since the ancestors died'" (2 Peter 3:3-4).

It was an uncertain time for the church. Many grew impatient, shortsighted. Did it matter how they behaved, they wondered, if Jesus wasn't coming back soon? They allowed their internal struggles and external opposition to drown out their deeper convictions and beliefs and went back to their old ways of life. They relapsed.

Of course this isn't something that only the early church struggled with. Shortsightedness gets the best of us, too. It causes us to lock in on the "right here and right now," where we allow our current circumstances, our present thoughts and feelings, or our desires to drown out our deeper convictions and beliefs. How we feel or what we want comes to undermine what we trust and know.

We know a person is made in the image of God, but goodness it would feel really good to cut them down right now. We know that generosity is a better way to live, but it's hard to let go of that money right now. We know that life is better shared and that we ought to be involved in a small-group community, but we are just so busy with other stuff right now. We know that what we are about to do is unhealthy and even destructive, we know that God has something far better in mind, but it would feel so good to settle for less right now, just this time. We know that God's divine power has given us everything we need, but it doesn't exactly feel that way right now. So we allow anxiety, worry, stress, lust, apathy, and despair to wreak havoc right here, right now. Our shortsightedness locks us in on these circumstances rather than on the deeper truths we are called to embody. Perseverance means holding steadfastly to the good news of Jesus Christ, defiantly clinging to it when circumstances try to push us away from it.

Wrestling and Enduring

In the Book of Philippians, the apostle Paul offers us a good case study on what it looks like to move past shortsightedness and live with perseverance. Paul wrote the Letter to the Philippians from a Roman prison, which was not a pleasant place to be. He was there because of his allegiance to Jesus, and he faced the possibility of being executed. Early in the letter Paul says to the Philippian church, "If I continue to live in this world, I get results from my work. But I don't know what I prefer. I'm torn between the two because I want to leave this life and be with Christ, which is far better. However, it's more important for me to stay in this world for your sake" (Philippians 1:22-24).

Scholars working to translate this passage from Greek to English have to work very hard to give it some coherence. In the original language it is a grammatical mess. In fact, many commentators suggest that Paul's emotional state is actually bleeding through into his writing here. In his commentary on this passage, Ralph Martin says, "The agitation of Paul's mind is clearly to be seen in the broken syntax of his writing."[6] Paul's words stem from a powerful inner struggle.

What this means is, Paul is being very honest here. We often work hard to make the Scriptures nice and neat, but make no mistake: Paul is wrestling with what is in front of him. He says that he would rather depart and be with Christ. This word for depart was a military term which meant to break camp, to pack up and move on. It was also a nautical term used to describe the releasing of a ship from its moorings. But Paul doesn't mean physically moving from the prison. He's speaking metaphorically about his own death.[7] When faced with his "right here," Paul would rather give up.

At the same time, all around this passage we see some incredible declarations about what Paul believes. In Philippians 1:6, Paul says to the church, "I'm sure about this: the one who started a good work in you will stay with you to complete the job by the day of Christ Jesus." Paul is honest about what is going on in his heart and his mind, sharing his inner conflict about if he'd prefer to continue living a hard Christian life or if it's better to just go ahead and die in order to be with Christ. Yet despite this anxiety, Paul also shows deep confidence that God is faithful—that God finishes what God starts.

In verse 10, Paul speaks about what he often refers to as "the day of Christ." This is the return of Christ that many had given up hope in by the time Second Peter was written. It is the coming day when Christ will return to set things right.

In verse 12, Paul even has the audacity to say that he believes that somehow God will use what has happened to him to advance the gospel. Paul believes in a God who wastes nothing.

All of this in the same chapter where Paul visibly wrestles with his own desires and what is better for the people of God. This is what Paul means when he says that he is torn. It's as if he has two voices speaking to him: his "right here," his present circumstances, thoughts, feelings, and emotions, and his faith in Christ, what he believes and trusts to be true. The question then becomes, which one is Paul going to allow to call the shots? From which place is Paul going to make his decisions?

After being brutally honest with us about his anxiety over his "right here," Paul goes on to say in 1:25-26, "I'm sure of this: I will stay alive and remain with all of you to help your progress and the joy of your faith, and to increase your pride in Christ Jesus through my presence when I visit you again." I'm sure of this: I will stay alive and remain. In other words, I will endure. I will persevere. I will keep on keeping on. Paul has the virtue of endurance—he remains confident in Christ and holds on to that power and that knowledge—and it enables him to stay steadfast even while he's in prison.

One of the reasons why we often struggle with perseverance is because we allow our "right here" to call the shots. This is when our present circumstances, feelings, and urges drive us to make decisions that contradict our convictions and beliefs. Perseverance isn't about acting like we don't have a "right here." It isn't about ignoring our anxieties or our temptations or acting like they aren't real, that they aren't difficult. Paul is honest about his "right here" and we ought to be as well. Endurance is about meeting these fears and struggles with what we know to be true, the good news of Jesus Christ.

I wonder what would happen if we did something like this every time we were faced with some sort of discouragement, doubt, or unhealthy urge. I wonder what would happen if we would take a time-out and question or challenge such hardships with what we know at our core is true.

If you're anything like me, it doesn't take much for me to start running around like Chicken Little screaming about how the sky is falling. Not too long ago, the bottom of our hot water heater rusted out and basically flooded several rooms of our house. It didn't take long for me to imagine my family and me living in a FEMA trailer in our front yard. In those moments when we are feeling overwhelmed and we want to give up, or we are feeling that urge and we want to give in, what if instead, in that moment, we challenged our challenges with what we know and believe is true? This is what Paul means in Second Corinthians when he says, "Our weapons that we fight with aren't human, but instead they are powered by God for the destruction of fortresses. They destroy arguments, and every defense that is raised up to oppose the knowledge of God. They capture every thought to make it obedient to Christ" (2 Corinthians 10:4-5). We take a time-out, and we challenge our challenges.

There's something else about perseverance to keep in mind. The fruit of perseverance isn't something that we can see day-to-day, but instead we see it from month to month and year to year. Of course, we aren't necessarily OK with that, are we? We live in a microwave culture, which is used to things happening instantly. If things are going to change in our lives, we want that change to happen immediately. And when it doesn't, we get discouraged.

That's not how maturity works. It isn't instantaneous. As we said above, it's a "long obedience in the same direction."

I think there are a few things that can help us with this.

Begin at the Beginning

First of all, we have to be OK with beginning at the beginning. See, some of us have a hard time with endurance because we can't really get started. Our maturity gap is huge, and we know that our spiritual lives need a ton of work. We might not even know where to start. Our first steps might seem to be so small that we might as well not even do them. Perseverance often involves taking those small steps, trusting that God's power is at work even in them. We have to be OK with beginning at the beginning.

It's like when I began to make my health a priority after years of neglect. I couldn't pick back up where I left off, even though I wanted to. I had to begin with easier stuff. That was hard. In my mind, I was still Personal Trainer Nick who could handle an intense workout. But in reality, I was Out-of-Shape Nick who struggled to do ten push-ups. I'll never forget that first workout back. I wanted to quit because I wasn't as in shape as I wanted to be, but I had to understand that was the whole point—I wasn't in shape. I had to be OK with beginning at the beginning. Plus the low-level workout I did do was better than the superman workout I didn't do.

That's why it's important to shoot for little victories wher get started. They can help you build up endurance or perse gradually. Like for me, it all started with my first cup of (decided to start drinking it black again. No cream, no sugar was something about the victory that came from making tha ꜱmall decision early in the morning that empowered me to make the next right decision.

Humility is important here. In humility, accept the fact that you aren't going to know what to do when you start this journey forward toward maturity. You are going to feel overwhelmed and in over your head for sure, but I promise you won't feel that way forever. Recognizing that can help you endure without getting discouraged.

Look Back

Another practice that will help us in our journey forward is actually to look backward regularly. I'm not talking about changing our minds; I'm talking about reflection. But it's important to keep a long view here. Remember, the kind of growth we are shooting for doesn't take place overnight, and so we can get frustrated comparing ourselves with where we have been recently. We'll often feel as if today has been no different than yesterday, and that will often be true. However, if we look back to where we were a few months or a year earlier, we will be blown away by God's work in us. That kind of recognition can renew our commitment, giving us perseverance in the journey that lies ahead. This is why I'm in the habit of journaling. Every few weeks I read over old entries. Time and time again, I am overwhelmed by God's faithfulness.

Better Together

One of the greatest gifts we have when it comes to growing in perseverance is each other. Not only can we help push one another forward when we are settling for less, we can also point out the growth we see in one another's lives. Often other people see how God is working in us before we do. So as a group, renew your commitment to lean on one another as you continue this study. It is my hope that you have already been doing this and seeing the benefits of it. Or if you happen to be doing this study on your own, do me a favor and each out to some friends. Make spiritual companionship a part of your relationships with them. What would happen if you carved out some time to talk about the things that actually matter, to push one another forward in the ways we've been talking about?

Value the Hard Work

Finally, we can recognize that the work of moving forward is valuable. Practicing the virtue of perseverance, or any of the others we've discussed, is in a way actually reaching the goal itself for a moment. So there's value in the journey, not just in the destination.

Really what is behind our shortsightedness, our struggle to endure and persevere, is that we underestimate the kind of work that God wants to do in us. This, once again, goes back to where this all started—with our faith. God doesn't just want to deal with our symptoms. God wants to take care of the sickness. God's power is there to enable us to participate in the divine nature. God isn't interested in simple behavior modification—God is out to give us a new nature. In order for that to happen we must learn to love the process or the journey toward maturity just as much as we long for the fruit of maturity.

We want the results, but how do we feel about the work? Perseverance is about learning to lean into the struggle of growing into people who instinctively do the right thing.

It's like with my kids. The things I really want for them aren't things that I can just gift-wrap and hand to them. They are things that they will have to learn along the way. My wife and I picked out four things that we have committed to speak over our children and we have been doing that since the day they were born: brave, wise, strong, and worth it. But it's the journey toward bravery, wisdom, strength, and worth that will enable them to become these things.

We tell my son that he is brave—in order for him to know that he is going to have to face his fears. I tell him that he is wise. Learning that is going to require him to make mistakes and learn from them. We tell our daughters that they are strong—but that is only something they will come to realize after they have faced adversity. We tell them that they are worth it—but painfully, we know that they will have to learn that from the heartache that comes from losing your worth and value in other people or things.

What I want more than anything for my kids isn't to protect them or to keep them from pain. I want to see them grow into healthy, mature human beings who are able to handle whatever life throws at them. What makes us think that God wants anything less for us? When we get that, endurance becomes easier to understand. In many ways it's necessary to face hardships, and to persevere through them, in order to move forward. Then James's words begin to make more sense: "My brothers and sisters, think of the various tests you encounter as occasions for joy" (James 1:2). We can consider our trials a pure joy, because we no longer see them simply as a threat to be avoided, but as an opportunity to grow.

In closing let me leave you with this:

You are brave. You can face your fears.

You are wise. You can learn from your mistakes.

You are strong. You can face adversity.

You are worth it. You are loved by God.

You can do this. You can endure, you can persevere. You can move forward. You want to know how I know? Because God's divine power has given us everything we need.

In Your Group

Study Philippians 1:20-26

Read Philippians 1:20-26 on the following page and consider how Paul struggles and the endurance that he exhibits. Consider the following questions as you read it, and answer them in the space provided:

1. What questions do you want to ask Paul based on this passage?
2. What does Paul struggle with, and what role does perseverance play in his struggle?
3. Where do you see Paul taking a short-term view in this passage, and where do you see him taking a long-term view?
4. What about this passage encourages you or challenges you?
5. How might Paul's wrestling and perseverance lead to self-control? What is the relationship between self-control and perseverance?

Philippians 1:20-26

[20]It is my expectation and hope that I won't be put to shame in anything. Rather, I hope with daring courage that Christ's greatness will be seen in my body, now as always, whether I live or die. [21]Because for me, living serves Christ and dying is even better. [22]If I continue to live in this world, I get results from my work. [23]But I don't know what I prefer. I'm torn between the two because I want to leave this life and be with Christ, which is far better. [24]However, it's more important for me to stay in this world for your sake. [25]I'm sure of this: I will stay alive and remain with all of you to help your progress and the joy of your faith, [26]and to increase your pride in Christ Jesus through my presence when I visit you again.

What Resonates With You?

What from this session resonates with you? You're probably getting the hang of this by now. How does the idea of endurance or perseverance encourage you, and how does it challenge you?

What encouraged you?

What challenged you?

Perseverance and the Maturity Gap

What are some of the things you tend to blame your lack of maturity on? In the space below, list some of the reasons you find yourself giving for a lack of spiritual maturity, for the existence of your maturity gap. How would taking responsibility for your spiritual growth necessitate endurance? How would it help produce endurance or perseverance?

What role does endurance, or perseverance play in closing your maturity gap? What can you do to move from one-time acts of self-governance to "long obedience in the same direction"? Look back at your answers from session 3 about places where you struggle with your appetites or desires, as well as your goals for moving forward in self-control. In the space below, write or draw how these things might translate to the virtue of perseverance, holding out and committing yourself to them over the long haul.

Shortsightedness

What form of shortsightedness tends to get the best of you? The "right here" or the "right now"? What is the difference between the two? In the space below, describe what circumstances you are currently dealing with that make perseverance difficult.

The short-term doesn't always have to work against the long-term. In the space below, describe what tools, people, or circumstances you have that can make perseverance easier. How can you draw upon them in order to sustain and strengthen yourself in the virtue of perseverance?

Forward Goals

How can you and your fellow group members push one another forward when it comes to perseverance? Write some goals that are attainable, but also challenging. The goal is to move forward! Describe how you and your group members will hold one another accountable and push one another ahead toward maturity.

What goals will help you move toward the virtue of perseverance?

Session 5
Godliness

The other night my wife and I were at a get-together with some friends. I was in the backyard with some of the guys, and one of them was showing us a project he had been working on. He called it his "grill shack." It is as awesome as it sounds. Basically, it's a building sort of like a pergola with a metal roof, which will house his grill and his smoker so that he can use them year-round. He and his wife are some of the most hospitable people I have ever met, and he has a real gift with charcoal. These get-togethers tend to happen at their house, and the grill shack would give them some new options for hosting.

We were all standing around looking at what will eventually be his grill shack, when one of the guys noticed a huge, eight-inch by eight-inch, twelve-foot-long beam lying on the ground. He pointed to the beam and said to me, "Hey, think you can pick that up?"

I'm a bigger guy and fairly strong, so that sort of question gets thrown my direction quite a bit. It has gotten me in trouble more than once.

A couple of the guys volunteered to spot me, and next thing I know I'm getting myself ready to pick up this several-hundred-pound wooden plank in some strange attempt to prove that I've still got it. I swear my wife has a sixth sense or something. It's like she can smell my "stupid," because as soon as she saw the commotion she knew that I was about to do something that I probably shouldn't do. She started yelling, "Nick, what are you doing?!"

She was too late. I am happy to say that I did lift up that beam. But sadly, I also realized that I don't "still have it" because I injured my back. Really badly. In fact, I wrote this very paragraph with a heating pad nestled on my lower back. Hopefully by the time you read it I will have recovered.

The injury was actually a re-injury from something that happened a couple of years ago, and this is at least the third time it's happened. When the injury first occurred, I was terrified that I had slipped a disc or something. But after going to the doctor I found out that it was a really bad strain, which is essentially a sort of tear in your muscle.

I spent some time with a physical therapist who explained to me that properly rehabbing this sort of injury was really important. If you didn't do thorough rehab, a re-injury would likely occur. The rehab process begins with rest, but eventually you have to deal with scar tissue. Scar tissue is fibrous material that forms around an injury site as your body tries to pull the soft tissue back together. The thing about scar tissue, though, is that it's never as strong or as flexible as the tissue it replaces. If you don't reduce the scar tissue as much as possible, it increases the likelihood that you'll injure the same area again.

There is only one way to deal with scar tissue, and that is through a deep-tissue massage. Don't let that word *massage* fool you. It's not pleasant. Deep-tissue massage is really just a code word for cruel and unusual punishment. The physical therapists had me hitting octaves I didn't know I was capable of reaching.

After a few sessions with them, the therapists gave me a hard little yellow ball and told me to lie on top of it and roll around in order to continue to break up the scar tissue. It was also less than pleasant. I think I did it once and then I conveniently "lost" said yellow ball, which is probably why I wrote this with a heating pad strapped to my back.

The virtue we will explore in this session, godliness, is a lot like deep tissue massage. When it comes to our journey forward toward spiritual maturity, we progress in pursuit of godliness. Closing our maturity gap not only requires endurance, that we keep on keeping on, but also that we actively pursue godliness. Godliness is about allowing the grace of God to penetrate deeper and deeper into our lives—to move beneath the surface and break up our scar tissue.

The Mystery of Godliness

The word for godliness in our passage in Second Peter is the Greek word *eusebia*, and it means proper respect for God, reverence, or devotion. It can also be translated as "piety" or "devoutness" in addition to "godliness." One commentator describes it like this: "*Godliness is no static, stained-glass word. It is active—kinetic obedience that springs from a reverent awe of God.*"[1] How do you like that? Godliness is obedience inspired by awe. In a sense, godliness is about actively and continually responding to the awesome grace of God in our lives.

The Book of First Timothy can help us understand more about the sort of godliness that Scripture envisions, as it draws a link between "the mystery of godliness" and the incarnation of Christ. In 1 Timothy 3:16, Paul writes, "Without question, the mystery of godliness is great." He then it goes on to quote what seems like an early church hymn or a poem:

He was revealed as a human,

declared righteous by the Spirit,

seen by angels,

preached throughout the nations,

believed in around the world,

and taken up in glory.

Let's look at this poem one section at a time. "He was revealed as a human, declared righteous by the Spirit" is a poetic way of saying that the God of the universe took on flesh and became one of us. By his resurrection he was declared righteous, or vindicated by the Spirit. And through his death and resurrection, Jesus Christ defeated everything that keeps us from being fully human.

It goes on to say that Jesus was "seen by angels" and "preached throughout the nations." This imagery of being seen and preached, or appearing and being announced, was often associated with Caesar in the Roman Empire. So one way to understand this part of the hymn is that it declares Jesus to be the true Lord, ruler over heaven and earth.

The poem finishes by saying that Jesus was "believed in around the world, and taken up in glory." The word *believe* involves personal trust and loyalty, so not only is Jesus Lord, but people are invited to experience and to trust the reality and benefit of his reign in this life and in the one to come.

In other words, the "mystery of godliness" is that God has rescued us, that Jesus is Lord, and that through faith we can know healing and wholeness, right here in this life as well as in the age to come. If that doesn't inspire awe and lead to obedience, I don't know what will!

Godliness is about responding to the boundless grace of God in the mystery of Jesus Christ. And godliness is continuing devotion. It's a response we make not just at the beginning of our life with God, but in an ongoing way—in a way that leads to pleasing God in every area of our life.

Our devotion to God, our continued response to God's grace, will change us. It will move us forward, because God's grace has a bit of an edge to it. God's grace meets us where we are and embraces us right there in the middle of our mess; but make no mistake: God's grace does not intend to leave us alone. We won't remain where grace found us but will be changed through its work in our hearts and lives.

Repentance and Responding to God's Grace

Repentance is an important aspect of godliness. An ongoing and diligent response to the awe-inspiring grace of God leads naturally to repentance. The more we respond to God in active obedience, inspired by reverence for God, the more we will find ourselves repenting, turning away from sin and changing our lives to be more like Christ.

I want us to turn to what may seem like an unlikely place for an example of godliness, keeping in mind the role of repentance and responding in reverence and obedience to God. Let's look at Jonah 3:1-10:

> ¹The LORD's word came to Jonah a second time: ²"Get up and go to Nineveh, that great city, and declare against it the proclamation that I am commanding you." ³And Jonah got up and went to Nineveh, according to the LORD's word. (Now Nineveh was indeed an enormous city, a three days' walk across.)

> ⁴Jonah started into the city, walking one day, and he cried out, "Just forty days more and Nineveh will be overthrown!" ⁵And the people of Nineveh believed God. They proclaimed a fast and put on mourning clothes, from the greatest of them to the least significant.

6When word of it reached the king of Nineveh, he got up from his throne, stripped himself of his robe, covered himself with mourning clothes, and sat in ashes. 7Then he announced, "In Nineveh, by decree of the king and his officials: Neither human nor animal, cattle nor flock, will taste anything! No grazing and no drinking water! 8Let humans and animals alike put on mourning clothes, and let them call upon God forcefully! And let all persons stop their evil behavior and the violence that's under their control!" 9He thought, Who knows? God may see this and turn from his wrath, so that we might not perish.

10God saw what they were doing—that they had ceased their evil behavior. So God stopped planning to destroy them, and he didn't do it.

Most of us know the Book of Jonah for what takes place in chapter 1, when the prophet is swallowed up by a huge fish after running away from God's call for him to carry a word of repentance to the wicked city of Nineveh. Chapter 1 is where all the special effects are, but chapter 3 holds a lot of power. This chapter captures how the people of Nineveh respond to the word from God in a really over-the-top way. The Book of Jonah is read in Jewish synagogues around the world on Yom Kippur, or the Day of Atonement. Part of the power that comes from reading this book on the Day of Atonement is that it shows the thorough, amazing repentance that the Ninevites undertake. These unlikely people demonstrate what a true and proper response to God's grace looks like.

In chapter 3, Jonah finally makes it to Nineveh, which was the capital city of the Assyrian Empire. The Assyrians were some of Israel's most powerful enemies, and they were one of the most feared and despised empires in world history. They were known for their ruthlessness, torturing and killing the people that they conquered. In 722 B.C., the Assyrians conquered the northern kingdom of Israel and deported much of its population. The Assyrians were a nasty bunch, which helps explain Jonah's reluctance to go to their capital city and deliver to them a message of repentance.

When the prophet finally does come to town, he delivers one of the shortest prophecies in the entire Bible. It's only nine words long in English, and only five words in the original Hebrew. Often when a prophet delivers a word from God it is several chapters long, but not

Jonah. Jonah rolls up and says to the people, "Just forty days more and Nineveh will be overthrown!"

Jonah here reminds me of when I was a teenager and my parents would ask me to do something I didn't want to do. Sure, I would do it, but I would make sure to do such a lousy job that they would never ask me again. When I first got married I did one load of laundry and "accidentally" shrunk one of Lindsey's favorite shirts. Guess who has never had to do laundry again? This is what I picture Jonah being like here in chapter 3. Sure, God, I'll deliver a word to the Ninevites. "Just forty days more and Nineveh will be overthrown!"

What's crazy though is that they respond to what seems like a half-hearted sermon in a really over-the-top sort of way. We are told that everyone, from the greatest to the least, even the animals, responded with an incredible demonstration of repentance. Despite his lackluster effort, Jonah is actually the most successful prophet in all of Scripture.

With their dramatic response of repentance, the Ninevites show us what godliness looks like in action. They come to revere God, and they act out of devotion and obedience. The first thing we can learn from the Ninevites is that their response was immediate. We are told that it would take about three days for Jonah to make his way through the whole city and preach his message (Jonah 3:3), but in verse 4 we are told that he actually walked only one day into the city. After just one day, Jonah's message spread like wildfire. Just one day of preaching, and at the end of it everyone, including the king, had heard the prophet's message and responded to it.

Responding Immediately

The Ninevites' repentance was immediate. There was no questioning, no rationalizing, no procrastinating, no committee meetings. The people heard the message, believed God, and responded to it with mourning and fasting throughout the city (Jonah 3:5). They exemplified a message we see the author of Hebrews lift up: "Today, if you hear his voice, don't have stubborn hearts" (Hebrews 3:7-8). They heard his voice and didn't resist, but immediately repented.

How do you respond when you feel that poke, that nudge, or that sense of conviction from God? When you get a sense there is something you need to do, or something you need to stop doing, what do you do? How quickly do you respond to it?

Often when you and I feel a sense of conviction about something, we have a tendency to put off responding to it. Maybe we try to drown it out, or maybe we simply rationalize it away. "God isn't telling me to do that." "It's not that big of a deal." "That's not God; I'm just feeling the effects of eating too much last night."

Today, when you hear God's voice don't have stubborn hearts. How do you respond to that voice?

Contrast the immediate response of the Ninevites with the response Jonah initially had to God's word. When Jonah first heard God telling him to go and deliver a message to the Ninevites, he tried to run as far away from them as possible. It's wild, the lengths we will go to avoid responding to God's grace in our lives.

The Book of Jonah challenges us, because it's the prophet, the religious insider, who runs away from God while the outsiders turn to God right away. If we're honest with ourselves, we must admit that far too often we respond as Jonah did. Sometimes we can experience what seems like a crisis of faith, which is actually just an attempt to ignore a sense of conviction. I saw this all the time working with high school and college-age students. Someone would come to me and say, "I'm not sure I can buy into all of this Jesus stuff anymore. I'm struggling with my faith." After a little exploration, it would become obvious that this person just wanted to be able to sleep with his or her girlfriend or boyfriend and not feel bad about it. The faith struggle was an attempt to run away from God.

Of course, this shows up in more areas than just romantic relationships. Whether it's with politics, issues of forgiveness, or how we spend our money, we hear that voice calling us to do something we don't want to do. And often when we hear it, we try to tune out that voice by tuning in to the voices that are easier for us to listen to. Then eventually God just so happens to be for all of the things we are for and against all of the people and things we are against, and just wants us to do whatever feels good.

Godliness, however, means hearing God's voice and responding with active obedience, inspired by reverence and appreciation of what God has done for us. It's not that we aren't free to question or wrestle with things—we are, and we should do that. But a life lived well is a life guided and directed by something bigger than our appetites and desires. Reverence, godliness, means recognizing that God is much, much bigger than we are, and living our lives as if that is true. I don't know about you, but I have found that just because I really want something doesn't mean it is good for me. A life lived well is a life that is centered on what we have discovered to be true, and for me the way of Jesus is the truest thing I know.

Ignoring or outright refusing a sense of God calling us to do something is only one way to turn away from it. There are also those of us who fully intend to respond to God's prompting, just not right now. We hear what God is saying, we know it's the right thing to do, and we fully intend to do the right thing. But just for right now, we are going to choose to do our own thing instead.

Here's the thing though, when it comes to godliness and responding to the grace of God: It isn't just a matter of what we are *doing* or *not doing*. This is a matter of who we are *becoming*. Remember, in life there is no neutral. The decisions we make move us in a particular direction. Even if we decide to do nothing, we are not standing still.

If you tune out the voice of God long enough, you may stop hearing it. Or even worse, you can develop scar tissue—you will harden your heart toward it altogether and it will start to seem oppressive to you. Sometimes a person gets caught up in something really destructive. There was a point in time when he knew it was wrong, that it was beneath him, but he has rationalized it so much that everything seems clouded now. Then someone who genuinely loves and cares for him has the guts to point it out, and he gets all defensive and writes the friend off as being judgmental. He comes to choose the destructive pattern over the person whom he should recognize as a loving friend who is on his side. If we don't respond to God's grace immediately, the danger is that we can actually stop seeing it as a gift and we begin to perceive it as a threat.

Responding Wholeheartedly

There's something else about the Ninevites' response to God: it was extraordinarily thorough. It was wholehearted. Jonah 3:5 tells us that everyone, from the greatest to the least, responded to Jonah's message with fasting and mourning clothes. Then when the king gets word, he decides to make the fast official. Here's where it gets a bit over the top. In verses 7-8, the king make a proclamation: "In Nineveh, by decree of the king and his officials: Neither human nor animal, cattle nor flock, will taste anything! No grazing and no drinking water! Let humans and animals alike put on mourning clothes, and let them call upon God forcefully! And let all persons stop their evil behavior and the violence that's under their control!"

You're kidding, right? The king calls a fast for everyone...even the animals. Not only that, he even tells the people to put sackcloth on the animals. Every creature in the city becomes involved in the fast, neither eating food nor drinking water, and puts on mourning clothes to show that they are repenting and seeking to turn back to God. The Ninevites' response to God was thorough, wholehearted.

The second half of verse 8 is especially interesting. Speaking to the people, the king says, "Let all persons stop their evil behavior and the violence that's under their control!" The sackcloth and fasting weren't entirely new things for the Ninevites. They were both fairly common religious practices in the ancient Near East. However, the king takes it a step further by telling the people to give up their wicked ways and the violence that is in their hands. There is movement from a general, somewhat typical religious ritual to a specific and very personal response that meant a drastic changing of the people's behavior.

I wonder how many of us struggle to experience any sort of lasting change in our lives because we have never moved past a general, sort-of-religious way of acting and way of thinking and into a personal commitment to live rightly in every area of our lives. There's always a risk of putting our response to God's grace in a sort-of-religious box. One's commitment to Jesus may influence a few general things like how we vote, what we are against, what we believe will happen to us after we die, and maybe how we spend a couple of hours on Sunday morning; but that's really about it. When we keep it in that sort-of-religious box, it doesn't really change much about how we live our daily lives and interact with other people. But true, thorough godliness involves our whole lives, every aspect of who we are.

When our pursuit of godliness isn't thorough, one of two things tends to happen. On the one hand, our commitment to Jesus can become situational. When things are bad, we are at the feet of Jesus, and we are willing to do whatever it takes to get our lives in order. We make big promises to God during times of crisis, but when things start to settle back to normal we drift right back to the way things were before. On the other hand, the opposite can happen. We turn away from God when things go badly for us. When things in our lives are good, things with God are good. But once it starts to get a little hairy, when something unexpected happens, or when something doesn't go our way, then we act as if God isn't holding up God's end of the bargain and we bail.

If our godliness isn't thorough, if this is what our faithfulness looks like, then nothing is ever really going to change in our hearts and lives. We will just find ourselves living in these monotonous cycles or repetitive peaks and valleys, and we will never actually move forward. We will never close the gap between our real and our ideal.

At the same time, when our pursuit of godliness isn't thorough, our faith will be shallow. When we first experience God's grace we are all-in; we can't get enough. But somewhere along the way, we get bored. We grow complacent. It all gets too familiar, and the more familiar we get with something the less we appreciate it. So often what happens is that we grow complacent, and we forget just how good the good news is. We lose that fresh encounter with God's grace and stop allowing it to work within us. We become blind to all of the places that we haven't let God's grace go deep enough—all of the things God still needs to rescue us from.

God may have rescued us from the big stuff, but what about the less obvious stuff? Godliness means opening yourself to God's grace so that the less obvious stuff becomes clear, and then obeying God to live well in those areas of your life, too.

The closer I get to Jesus, the more convinced I am that I need him. It's like when you are wearing a dark shirt; the closer you get to a light, the more stuff shows up on it. When I first really started following Jesus, I made some big lifestyle changes. Now the changes I need to make aren't as drastic; but I'll be honest, they sting a bit more. Now I sense God calling me to pay attention to things like my motives and the reasons behind why I do what I do. These things are deeper than surface-level behaviors. But godliness means motives and reasons that are devoted to God, not just actions alone.

Grace isn't just something we needed a long time ago when this whole faith thing got started in our lives. It's something we need on a daily basis in order to grow more and more into the people God created us to be. This constant experience of God's grace empowers us to respond more and more thoroughly to God's presence in our lives.

Trusting God to Do Great Things

For most of us, this talk about pursuing godliness can at times, or most of the time, seem overwhelming. It's difficult for us to believe that we can actually know godliness. Some of us live with this profound sense of frustration with ourselves because we can't seem to turn the corner. I want to once again remind you where all of this starts: with our faith in the saving love of God.

The author of First John says, "See what kind of love the Father has given to us in that we should be called God's children, and that is what we are!" (1 John 3:1). John is fired up here—you can tell by the exclamation marks. It's as if he is shouting this at us, and he is shouting it because he knows it's not the only voice we hear. There's also the voice of condemnation and guilt that keeps us stuck in our mess. But over and against that voice we have the voice of truth saying to us, "That's not who you really are—you are loved—you are a child of God!"

Then in verse 2, John goes on to say, "Dear friends, now we are God's children, and it hasn't yet appeared what we will be. We know that when he appears we will be like him because we'll see him as he is." God is up to something in us. God is at work, and we aren't always sure what God is up to. But we can be sure that God is working in us, and when God is finished working in us we will be like Christ. Now that's a verse that belongs on a coffee mug—a very big coffee mug. What we will be has not yet been made known. But we know that when Christ appears we shall be like him. Pursuing godliness means responding to God's grace with obedience and trust, inspired by the great power of Christ and the great love of God.

This reminds me of when I went to get a tattoo. I had a really big piece in mind that I wanted to have put on my forearm. It was a cover-up of some Japanese characters that I had picked from a wall in a tattoo shop when I was nineteen. That's a whole other story. But for this one, I took my time putting the piece together, and then I spent a lot of time researching the right artist. Everyone kept pointing me to a guy named Matt. I checked out some of his work, and I was blown away. This guy was good. So I made an appointment with him and gave him an idea of what I wanted. He went and drew something up, and of course it was way better than what I had originally envisioned.

When the time came for our first session, I was so excited to see it all come together. But not long after Matt got started, I began to get a little nervous. I had no idea what he was doing, and I didn't understand why he was going about it the way he was. He was drawing lines over here and shading stuff over there, and it just didn't make any sense. I remember thinking to myself, "You know you can't just erase this, right?" So I started asking him a bunch of questions about what he was doing, and I'm sure I got on his nerves. But I remember at one point looking down at my arm and thinking, "OK, you have no idea what he is doing—it makes no sense to you—but you do know the artist. You have seen his work. You know what he can do, and he has shown you the finished product. Even though you have no idea why he is going about it this way, you can be sure that when he's done it will be amazing." I didn't understand the process, but I trusted the artist and let him work.

What we will be has not yet been made known. But we know that when Christ appears we shall be like him...

Godliness means trusting and obeying God, responding to God's saving love by allowing it to go deeper and deeper into your heart and life. If you have said yes to the saving love of God, then here's what you can be sure of: God is up to something in you. God is at work. We don't always see it, and it doesn't always make sense, but we do know the artist. We have seen his work. We know the finished product. When God is finished with us, it's going to be amazing.

In Your Group

Study Jonah 3:1-10

Read Jonah 3:1-10 on the following page. Think about the Ninevites' godliness, and Jonah's lack of it. Consider the following questions as you read the passage, and answer them in the space provided:

1. What questions do you have as you read this passage?
2. What motivates the Ninevites' godliness? Why does Jonah not respond in the same immediate, thorough manner as they do?
3. What evidence of godliness do you see in the people of Nineveh? How do their words, actions, or attitudes express godliness?
4. What about this passage encourages you or challenges you?
5. Where do you see the other virtues we have discussed— goodness, knowledge, self-control, and perseverance—come to play among the Ninevites? What does this say about godliness?

Jonah 3:1-10

¹The Lord's word came to Jonah a second time: ²"Get up and go to Nineveh, that great city, and declare against it the proclamation that I am commanding you." ³And Jonah got up and went to Nineveh, according to the Lord's word. (Now Nineveh was indeed an enormous city, a three days' walk across.)

⁴Jonah started into the city, walking one day, and he cried out, "Just forty days more and Nineveh will be overthrown!" ⁵And the people of Nineveh believed God. They proclaimed a fast and put on mourning clothes, from the greatest of them to the least significant.

⁶When word of it reached the king of Nineveh, he got up from his throne, stripped himself of his robe, covered himself with mourning clothes, and sat in ashes. ⁷Then he announced, "In Nineveh, by decree of the king and his officials: Neither human nor animal, cattle nor flock, will taste anything! No grazing and no drinking water! ⁸Let humans and animals alike put on mourning clothes, and let them call upon God forcefully! And let all persons stop their evil behavior and the violence that's under their control!" ⁹He thought, Who knows? God may see this and turn from his wrath, so that we might not perish.

¹⁰God saw what they were doing—that they had ceased their evil behavior. So God stopped planning to destroy them, and he didn't do it.

What Resonates With You?

What from this session resonates with you? How does the reflection on godliness encourage you, and how does it challenge you? Remember: Places where we resist the message or key ideas are opportunities to grow. So name and recognize where those challenges are, as well as the places of encouragement that you find!

What encouraged you?

What challenged you?

The Pursuit of Godliness

How would you describe the pursuit of godliness in your own words? Why is it so important in our journey toward maturity? How does it relate to the other virtues we have discussed so far? What might godliness look like in your life? Write your thoughts in the space below.

Immediate and Thorough Response

Why is it important for our response to God's grace to be immediate? In the space below, identify situations or areas in your life where God might be calling out to you, seeking for you to respond in some way. What will it mean for you to respond immediately? What is at stake if you wait?

Why is it important for our response to God's grace to be thorough? In the space provided, list places or aspects of your life where God's grace needs to penetrate more deeply, changing you in deeper ways. As you reflect, recall above the idea that the more we come to know God, the more we see that we are in need of transformation.

Forward Goals

How can you and your small group members push one another forward when it comes to pursuing godliness? Make a list of goals that you can set and commit to in order to go further in the virtue of godliness. As with the other virtues, identify goals that are practical and attainable but that will also challenge you. Be sure also to list the ways that you and your fellow group members can support one another and push one another forward.

What goals will help you move toward the virtue of godliness?

Session 6
Mutual Affection

L ife is better shared.

A couple of years ago I had to endure my first mom's day out. Have you heard of these? It's when a group of moms decide to plan a day out and leave the dads at home on their own with the kids... all by themselves.

To be completely honest, I was looking forward to this particular afternoon with a good bit of dread. Sure, the quality time with the kids was a good thing, but the responsibility piece had me all worked up. I had to make sure that no one got lost or seriously injured for an entire afternoon by myself. The plan was simple: I would barricade us in the house, and we would just hold down the fort and wait it out until Mom got home.

Now my wife planned this wonderful little excursion with several other moms whose husbands were on staff with me at the church where I served. They tried to make it as easy as possible on us, so they scheduled it for a Sunday. This meant that by the time we picked the kids up from children's ministry after worship, it would really be more like an afternoon on our own instead of a whole day. My friend James Keith was the worship pastor at the church, and his wife was also in on the mom's day out. James and I ran into each other picking up the kids after worship, and it was clear by the look on our faces we were both anxious about the afternoon in front of us. When it was time to go our separate ways, we promised to pray for one another. We left church looking like a couple of pack mules, draped with diaper bags and kids hanging all over us.

I was able to get the kids loaded up in the van, and I was about to pull out of the parking lot when James pulled up next to me. He rolled down his window and said, "Want to go to lunch?" Now on one hand I was thinking, "That sounds like an awful idea. Just stick to the plan, stay in the house, and nobody gets hurt." But on the other hand, I thought, "Why not?" As small and brainless of a thought as that is, it has a history of winning out when I'm in an internal debate with myself. So we went to lunch.

Now just picture two dads, armed with their diaper bags, taking six kids out to eat on a Sunday afternoon. The funny thing is, the restaurant where we ate was virtually empty when we got there. It makes me think they all saw us coming in the parking lot and ran out the back.

I definitely didn't stick to the plan that day. After we finished lunch, we ended up spending the rest of the afternoon together. We even ended up at one of those enormous indoor entertainment centers that has wall-to-wall arcade games, bumper cars, and a room full of inflatable jump houses. We shut the place down that night!

I'm proud to say that we survived and nobody got hurt. Yeah, sure, we did forget to feed the kids dinner, but that's nothing a couple of late-night Pop Tarts can't fix, right? It was messy, crazy, and really exhausting, but at the same time it was a ton of fun.

It just goes to prove the point: As messy as it can be, life is just better shared. Wouldn't you agree?

I bring this up because the next virtue in our list from 2 Peter 1 is affection for others, and it has very much to do with our shared life with one another. These three English words, affection for others, are a translation of one Greek word, *philadelphia* (any Eagles fans out there?). It literally means "brotherly love" or "love of brothers"— the word is actually a combination of the words *phileo,* love, and *adelphos,* brother—which is why today Philadelphia is known as the city of brotherly love. As it's used here, "affection for others" or "mutual affection" (NIV) captures the word's meaning pretty well.

Mutual Affection

In our culture, we usually tend to think of love in the romantic sense. But that's not primarily what the Greek word *phileo* conveys. Phileo is one of several words in the Greek language that are translated into our word *love*. Each word has its own nuance, and phileo doesn't necessarily refer to romance but to the kind of love that is at the core of a really good friendship.

There is another Greek word, *storge,* that describes the natural, almost effortless affection we have for the people close to us, most often family relationships and especially of parents for children. It's that unforced sense of warmth and kindness we feel toward some of our favorite people—the ones we can't help but be fond of.

The kind of love envisioned by philadelphia is bit more involved than that. It requires intentionality and even a good bit of effort at times on our part. That is why it is often translated as "mutual affection" as the NIV translates it in 2 Peter 1:7. It is the love that exists within purposeful friendships of mutual obligation, where there is genuine concern for one another's growth into healthy human beings.

The author of Second Peter calls us to add to our faith philadelphia, mutual affection, in our journey forward toward maturity.

There are two sides to this. On the one hand, if we are moving forward in our faith—in our life with God—we will also be growing in kindness and grace toward other people. First John 4:19-21 puts it pretty bluntly: "We love because God first loved us. If anyone says, I love God, and hates a brother or sister, he is a liar, because the person who doesn't love a brother or sister who can be seen can't love God, who can't be seen. This commandment we have from him: Those who claim to love God ought to love their brother and sister also." This maturity thing is not some individualistic morality that plays out in isolation. We cannot separate our life with God from our relationships with the people around us. The clearest indicator of the health of our connection with God is the health of our connections with others. If your religious ideologies lead you to be a jerk, then your religious ideologies aren't Christian and quite frankly they aren't very helpful either. Affection for others is on the one hand a fruit of our faith—it is something that we grow in as we press more and more into God's saving love.

On the other hand, the author tells us to add to or supplement our faith with mutual affection, which means it's also something that will help us in our life of forward movement. Our journey forward is nothing we do on our own. It is something that is going to require us to lean on one another to be and do more than we ever could on our own. Mutual affection is both a fruit of our faith and a must-have tool for our growth toward spiritual maturity.

Mutual affection is difficult for us for both of those reasons. Not everyone is easy for us to love, so as a goal it's a challenge to reach. And at the same time, in a culture obsessed with independence, it can be hard to receive philadelphia from others, so we don't have easy access to it as a tool. This twofold difficulty makes it doubly important that we develop this virtue purposefully, making mutual affection a key area of our spiritual maturity.

Don't Judge

In order to get some more insight on this virtue, we are going to turn to one of the more famous teachings of Jesus found in the Gospel of Matthew.

The Gospel of Matthew is often referred to as the Gospel of the church. There are various reasons for this, but one is that it's the only Gospel of the four that actually uses the word *church*. One of the author's intentions in writing Matthew was to help the early church understand its identity in light of the life, death, and resurrection of Jesus—particularly in regard to how they were to live and interact with each other. That's why all throughout the Gospel you will find teachings from Jesus specifically directed at our relationships with one another in the Christian community.

In Matthew 7, as part of the Sermon on the Mount (Matthew 5–7), we find one of Jesus' more famous teachings: "Don't judge, so that you won't be judged. You'll receive the same judgment you give. Whatever you deal out will be dealt out to you." (Matthew 7:1-2). This has got to be one of the most quoted teachings of Jesus. Even people who don't identify as Christian will draw upon a version of this verse from time to time. It's likely there has been a time when someone has quoted this to you, or when you have quoted it to someone else. But, like many oft-quoted sayings, people often misunderstand it and misuse it. Frequently *judge* is used as a synonym for *criticize,* so "don't judge" is a code for "don't criticize." But that's not quite what Jesus has in mind. Perhaps the first thing we need to do, then, is to try to understand more fully what Jesus meant when he said, "Don't judge."

The Greek word for judge is *krino,* and it is a common word in the New Testament that gets used in a couple of different ways. On the one hand, *krino* can mean "to make a decision about something." So you *krino*-ed when you decided what to have for breakfast this morning.

But surely this can't be what Jesus is talking about in Matthew 7. The word is also used to refer to making a more official judgment that would take place in a courtroom setting. It can mean "to judge or decide in a judicial process." Or it can mean "to think or consider," making a decision or selection after considering various factors. These aren't what Jesus is talking about either. It's a word with a wide range of meanings, so it's important that we identify what specific meaning of *judge* Jesus has in mind.

An instance of the word that shows up in 1 Corinthians 4:5 helps bring some clarity to what Jesus is talking about in Matthew. In 1 Corinthians 4:5 Paul, the author, says, "So don't judge anything before the right time—wait until the Lord comes. He will bring things that are hidden in the dark to light, and he will make people's motivations public. Then there will be recognition for each person from God." Here judging is associated with uncovering or revealing someone's motives. To judge someone, then, is to make a decision or to draw a conclusion about the essence or the core of who someone is. Tell me, according to this passage, whose job is it to judge in this sort of way? Certainly not ours. It's God's job. James says it even more clearly when he writes that there is only one judge, and it's God (see James 4:12).

When Jesus says to us "Don't judge," this is what he is talking about. It is the tendency you and I have to make decisions about someone based upon a limited view of them. We often do it to try to elevate ourselves at the expense of one another. Think about it: Usually when we draw negative conclusions about someone's inner core or motives, we do it to feel better about ourselves.

If you are having a hard time identifying what this looks like in our lives, I'll go first. I love to people-watch. It may be one of my favorite things to do. This is going to sound really shallow, and it is, but this is a confession so you're not allowed to krino me. I am getting honest here in the hopes that you will then have the guts to be honest as well, so here it goes . . .

Every June my family spends a week at a beach in North Carolina, and one of the reasons why I love this beach so much is because, believe it or not, I am one of the most in-shape people there—don't judge me! Well, while I'm sitting around the pool or at the beach, I love to watch people. As I'm doing it, there is a running commentary going through my head about them. It usually starts off all nice and friendly, but it doesn't take long for it to turn a bit ugly. I start thinking things like, "I can't believe she is wearing that bathing suit out here...obviously she doesn't have any friends." Or, "Oh look at Mr. Tuff Guy over there in the Tap Out graphic tee—I bet I could take him." My favorite, though, now that I'm a dad is, "I can't believe they are letting their kid do that—what kind of parents are they?" And all the while, my son is right next to me drinking a tube of sunscreen.

I'm sure you can relate to this. This is what Jesus is talking about when he says, "Don't judge." It can be easy to blow off something like that and think, "Oh what's the big deal, you didn't say any of it out loud." Actually, it is a big deal, because for one it isn't very long until I am saying it out loud and I'm bringing my wife in on it. And what's more, these thoughts are shaping my character. Remember, there is no neutral in life. Every judgmental thought I have, even if I don't voice it, turns me into a more judgmental person. And my virtue of affection for others diminishes.

When we judge other people, we blur the line between their behavior and their identity. We confuse *who they are* with *what they are doing* or what they have done. We make these sweeping generalizations and assumptions about people we actually know very little about. For instance, there's a kid on our child's soccer team who is a bit more rambunctious than the other kids and has a tendency to get in trouble, and we start making judgments about his parents. Or a couple gets a divorce, and everyone starts making assumptions about whose fault it is. Or we see a person using food stamps at the grocery store, and we immediately put a mental label on them. We assume things about their work ethic while we remain blind to various privileges that have been handed to us.

This is judging. This is krino. It is when we blur the line between what someone does and who they are as a person. Jesus has a big problem with it and his teaching is clear: Don't do it! Don't judge. It's not helpful, and it's not our job. At the same time, krino is one of the biggest obstacles for you and me to overcome if we are going to grow in a virtue of mutual affection. Think about it. Mutual affection is about being in the kind of relationships where we are truly and genuinely concerned with helping one another grow forward. Judging one another is the complete opposite of that. When we judge, we aren't concerned with pushing someone forward. We are concerned with elevating ourselves at the other's expense. So once again, the question becomes how do we move past it? Well, let's keep reading in Matthew 7.

Seeing Yourself Honestly

After instructing us not to judge, Jesus says,

> ³Why do you see the splinter that's in your brother's or sister's eye, but don't notice the log in your own eye? ⁴How can you say to your brother or sister, 'Let me take the splinter out of your eye,' when there's a log in your eye? ⁵You deceive yourself! First take the log out of your eye, and then you'll see clearly to take the splinter out of your brother's or sister's eye.
>
> (Matthew 7:3-5)

This imagery from Jesus is meant to be funny. Jesus is telling a joke and making a profound point. The picture is of someone with a massive plank—imagine the big wooden beam from the grill shack that I hurt my back trying to lift. Someone has this huge thing in his eye, and he is walking around pointing out everyone else's speck of dirt.

Jesus says that the first thing that has to happen to move past krino is to remove the plank. Like with any healthy movement in our lives, moving forward in terms of mutual affection begins with a healthy dose of self-awareness.

Often, the people who bother us the most make the best mirrors. When we find ourselves really fired up and angry toward a certain person or group of people, our first instinct is to lash out and go on the attack. I suggest instead, we ought to take a step back and do some self-examination. What is it in me that is fueling this anger and resentment? Is there some sort of unresolved issue in my own life that makes it really hard for me to extend grace and forgiveness? Perhaps we react so strongly to the splinter of wood in our neighbor's eye precisely because we have a plank in our own. We aren't very quick to do this, are we? It's hard to do. We aren't very good at taking responsibility for our feelings about other people. We typically think that how we are feeling and thinking is a justified response to what "they" have done or keep doing. But sometimes it has more to do with what we haven't allowed God to do in us.

First Corinthians 10:12-13 says, "So those who think they are standing need to watch out or else they may fall. No temptation has seized you that isn't common for people." The same brokenness that we love to point out, judge, and condemn in other people lives in us as well. God help us if we ever forget that. That's the real danger with our planks. Not only do they look ridiculous, they keep us from dealing with our own dysfunction, so we never fully experience the healing that we need. The people who bother us the most make the best mirrors. They can be an opportunity for us to get a clearer picture of ourselves and to identify the things we still need God to make right.

Seeing One Another Clearly

Moving past krino and toward phileo will certainly require self-reflection, which is about seeing ourselves honestly. It will also require us to see one another truly as well. It's interesting in this teaching that Jesus keeps referring to the person with the speck as the other person's brother or sister. In verse 3, "Why do you see the splinter that's in your brother's or sister's eye..." Verse 4, "How can you say to your brother or sister..." Then at the end of verse 5, "and then you'll see clearly to take the splinter out of your brother's or sister's eye." It's like Jesus wants to be clear who we are talking about here: your brother or your sister. It seems that people with the plank no longer see the person in front of them because they have become so fixated on the speck and now the speck is all they see. But remember: Philadelphia, mutual affection, is "brotherly love." We can't truly experience this virtue without recognizing our neighbor as family.

There is a really beautiful encounter that takes place in Luke 13 between Jesus and a woman who had been crippled by a spirit for eighteen years.

> [10]Jesus was teaching in one of the synagogues on the Sabbath.
> [11]A woman was there who had been disabled by a spirit for
> eighteen years. She was bent over and couldn't stand up
> straight. [12]When he saw her, Jesus called her to him and said,
> "Woman, you are set free from your sickness." [13]He placed his
> hands on her and she straightened up at once and praised God.
>
> (Luke 13:10-13)

The woman's disease had left her bent over. The text tells us that she had been "disabled by a spirit," but other than that we are not really given much of an explanation in terms of the origin of her suffering. One thing we can be sure of, though, is that in her world she was on the outside looking in.

In the ancient world, physical illness like this carried with it social consequences. The assumption would have been that either the woman or someone related to her had done something terribly wrong. She or a relative had committed some sort of heinous sin, and this illness was a form of divine justice. She would have been identified as unclean and been forced to live in isolation.

In light of this reality, verse 12 is quite beautiful. It says, "When he saw her, Jesus called her to him and said, 'Woman, you are set free from your sickness.'" Note the first part of that verse: "When he saw her." You have to wonder how long it had been since anyone had truly looked at *her*. Jesus knows that there is more to this woman than the overly simplistic categories and labels the world has slapped on her. Quite simply, Jesus looks at her through the eyes of compassion and knows that there is a story behind her illness. No one wakes up one morning and decides they want to live this woman's life; things happened to get her there. Jesus saw her. He saw more than her speck—he saw her.

That is our challenge if we are to embrace philadelphia, mutual affection, as a virtue in our journey forward. We have to see, really see, people through compassionate eyes.

We all have people in our lives who are hard to love. There are people who drive us nuts, and the very thought of them makes our eyes roll in the back of our head. We just don't understand them; they don't play by our rules; they are intrusive and annoying; and they get under our skin. Maybe it's a co-worker, maybe it's a family member, or a neighbor, or the parent of one of your child's friends. Or it could be a whole group or tribe of people. Let me ask you, how much do you know about them? How much do you know about their story, why they are the way they are? What do you know about how they were raised or what their family life was like? What do you know about what they have to go home to every day? C. S. Lewis once said, "There are no *ordinary* people. You have never talked to a mere mortal."[1] He is referring to the fact that everyone you meet has been created in the image of God, which means they are of untold worth and value. Think about how much would change, in our lives and in the world in general, if we could somehow see other people for more than their specks.

I had the honor of serving as what is called the pastor of record for a man on death row. Our relationship began with letter writing, but eventually I started meeting with him in person. I remember our first visit. The whole morning leading up to it was really unnerving. He had committed a truly heinous crime, and I had no idea what to expect about our meeting. What was I supposed to say to him? The process of getting into the prison was especially disturbing. I showed up right at a shift change, so there was all of this commotion as some guards were on their way out and others were on their way in. It was loud and busy and it was all unfamiliar. I had to go through a couple of different metal detectors, and I was led through several different gates and locked doors. All the while I began to feel more and more uneasy about the whole thing. That prison was one of the few places I have been in my life where it seemed like the presence of God wasn't there.

As they led me farther and farther into that prison, God felt further and further away...until I sat down across from the man I'd come to meet. I have never seen so much peace in an individual in my entire life. Yes, he had done some really awful things. He knew that, and he had come to terms with it. But it was evident that he knew Jesus, and he was different because of it. See, I thought I was leaving Jesus in the parking lot, but the truth is I met Jesus in the belly of that prison in a man who had been radically transformed by God's grace. God's grace doesn't play by our rules, and it certainly doesn't confuse our identity with our behavior. That prison was a great big speck, and at first it was all I could see. But when I met this man, I actually saw him. I was moved to brotherly love toward him.

Mutual Affection and Spiritual Maturity

Now this isn't where Jesus' teaching stops, but I sure wish it did. This is only that first side of mutual affection, but remember there is another side to it as well. Not only is it a fruit of our faith, it is also a tool for maturity. Notice what Jesus says in verse 5: "You deceive yourself! First take the log out of your eye, and then you'll see clearly to take the splinter out of your brother's or sister's eye." Here's where we see the other side of phileo/affection. Jesus believes that somehow, by the grace of God, you and I can become the kind of people who can actually help one another grow forward. The whole point of us removing our logs is so that we can help each other with our splinters.

This is something that I talked about a lot in my previous study, *One*. Jesus expects you and me to be in the kind of relationships where this sort of thing happens on a regular basis. Jesus wants us to be so grounded in grace, humility, and truth that we can come to one another and lovingly point out the things in each other's lives that are less than God's best.

Now keep in mind, we are only fit to do this once we have removed our log—once we have done some soul-searching, checked our motives, and are sure that we are doing the right thing. I don't know about you, but to me log removal feels rough and unwieldy. Not like removing a speck from someone's else's eye—that's delicate. The imagery of taking a speck from someone's eye reminds me of trying to take a splinter out of one of my kids' fingers. Parents, you know the only way you are going to get that splinter out is if the kid lets you—unless you have a straitjacket or something, that is. The relationships where we can do this sort of delicate work are relationships that are founded on trust, where it is clear that we truly want what is best for one another. Those relationships are characterized by mutual affection, the virtue of *philadelphia*.

Do you have that? I have found that it is rare. Sometimes our friends can be so close that they will stick up for us even when they shouldn't. This what separates *phileo* from that other word for love, *storge*. *Storge* is the kind of love that comes naturally and is effortless, but phileo involves intentionality and mutual obligation. Sometimes what we need more than anything is for someone to call us out—to speak the hard word. I know that is what I need! What I need is a group of people who are going fight for my marriage; who are going to come alongside me in the struggle to raise my kids; who are going to push me to be who I know God has called me to be. Do you have that? Because if you don't, you aren't going to make it.

There are several ways we can go with all of this.

Maybe there is someone, or a group of someones, you have labeled, judged, sized up and written off. What you need is the grace to do some self-reflection. What is it in you that is so threatened by them? Ask God to help you see and remove the log from your own eye. Ask God to give you the grace you need to do some soul-searching so that you can see them for more than their speck.

Or perhaps there is something you have noticed in the life of someone you care about. You know it isn't right, but you haven't said anything. Here's the deal: Your silence isn't doing them any good. We tell ourselves that the reason we aren't speaking up is because we don't want to hurt them, but that really isn't true. The reason we aren't speaking up is because we don't want to be uncomfortable. What you need is the grace to speak up and say the hard thing, because chances are they have been waiting for someone to say something.

Or there is a chance that somebody has actually come to you, out of love, and they have pointed out your speck and you wrote them off as being judgmental. There is a good chance their timing or delivery could have been off, but if you are honest you knew they were right. What you need is the grace to receive that word from them. To hear it and then to have the courage to do something about it.

Just like everything else in our journey forward toward maturity this mutual affection thing isn't easy, but I can assure you it is totally worth it. As messy as it is, life is way better shared.

In Your Group

Study Matthew 7:1-5

Read Matthew 7:1-5 on the following page, Jesus' instruction not to judge and the explan; it. Consider the following questions as you read the passag answer them in the space provided:

1. What do you want to know more about as you read this passage? What would you want to ask Jesus?
2. How do you think Jesus' audience reacted to his words? Why?
3. In what way does affection for others help us avoid judging? Or how is judging others an obstacle to mutual affection? What about this passage encourages you or challenges you?
4. What is the relationship between focusing on our own big issues (logs) and helping our neighbors with their issues (specks)? How do we challenge one another without judging?

"Don't judge, so that you won't be judged. ²You'll receive the same judgment you give. Whatever you deal out will be dealt out to you. ³Why do you see the splinter that's in your brother's or sister's eye, but don't notice the log in your own eye? ⁴How can you say to your brother or sister, 'Let me take the splinter out of your eye,' when there's a log in your eye? ⁵You deceive yourself! First take the log out of your eye, and then you'll see clearly to take the splinter out of your brother's or sister's eye."

What Resonates With You?

What from this session resonates with you? How does the reflection on mutual affection encourage you, and how does it challenge you? Remember: Places where we resist the message or key ideas are opportunities to grow. So name and recognize where those challenges are, as well as the places of encouragement that you find!

What encouraged you?

What challenged you?

Toward Spiritual Maturity

What exactly is mutual affection, and what role(s) does it play in our life of forward momentum? What makes it different from other types of love? In the space below, write the ways in which you have experienced this type of affection and how it has helped you grow toward Christ. How has experiencing this mutual affection helped move you toward maturity?

Don't Judge

Put it in your own words: What did Jesus mean in Matthew 7 when he said, "Don't judge?" What does judging look like in today's world?

Even though Jesus said it, we still tend to do it, don't we? How does this show up in your life? List the ways in which you tend to judge others. Then list the ways in which you have felt judged. How do Jesus' words give you a challenge and a word of comfort?

Seeing Clearly

On page 121, I said that the people who bother us the most often make the best mirrors. What does this mean? Do you find this to be true in your life? In the space below, describe how turning a critical eye toward ourselves first can help us avoid judging. How can seeing ourselves clearly help us grow in mutual affection?

Forward Goals

How can you and your fellow group members push one another forward when it comes to growing in mutual affection? How can you create the kind of atmosphere in your relationships that allows you to help one another with your specks? List some practical, attainable, challenging goals to help you move forward together. And identify ways you can hold one another accountable to this vision.

Maybe you're not in a small group and what you need to do now is go, gather some friends, and bring some intentionality into your relationships. Set that goal, and reach for it! You may wish to use the study *One: A Small Group Journey Toward Life-Changing Community* to help you get started.

What goals will help you move toward mutual affection?

Session 7
Love

Not long after my wife and I were married, we realized that there was something we forgot to hash out during our premarriage counseling: what to do with the brown La-Z-Boy recliner. Or, as Lindsey refers to it, "that ugly thing you call a chair." I'm pretty sure our first argument as a married couple had something to do with where to put it. In my mind it was obvious: The chair belonged in the same room as the television, preferably right in front of it. In her mind, the only reasonable thing to do was to take the chair out back and light it on fire. So we compromised and put the chair out in the garage. The house that we live in now has a basement, so thankfully the chair is once again back in business.

That chair looks pretty rough. It's beaten up, the fabric is ripped in places, it has some curious looking stains, and some of the frame is sticking out of the back. Even so, there is no way I could get rid of that chair because to me it's way more than a chair. It has been a part of my life for ten years. The brown chair was the only piece of furniture I owned when I moved out of my parents' house. For several years, I lived in a house with a bunch of guys, and in that house the brown chair was sacred. It was our power chair. There were several altercations over who was worthy enough to sit in it when a football game was on. Some of the best times in my life occurred in that house, and somehow those memories attached themselves to that chair. (That's probably why it smells a little funny.) In fact, I remember sitting in that chair after my first date with Lindsey, trying to explain to my best friend what was going through my head and how I was feeling.

What at first seemed like a simple problem of where to put an old piece of furniture ended up being way more complicated, way more involved than a home decorating issue. It was about how a tangible reminder of the good things from years past would fit into the new life I was making with my spouse. *This* was really about *that*.

Our journey toward spiritual maturity, our life forward, similarly has much more to it than what's apparent at first. We think it's just about *this*, when in fact, it's about *that*. Up to this point, it would be easy for us to think that our spiritual maturity is simply about our own personal life with God. But with this last virtue from Second Peter 1, we begin to see the bigger, deeper picture. We begin to understand that our movement forward is actually about so much more.

Love Is the Destination

The final virtue in our list from Second Peter is love. In the Greek it is the word *agape*. For the Scripture writers, this word represents the epitome of all Christian virtues. In Colossians 3, Paul shares another list of virtues and there, in verse 14, he says, "And over all these things put on love, which is the perfect bond of unity." Love is what this whole maturity thing is about. In our life of forward movement, love is the destination, the direction we are supposed to be headed in.

We need to be clear on what we mean when we say love, because *love* is a word that we get a lot of mileage out of in our culture. We tend to throw that word around an awful lot, without even thinking about it. Just the other day I was having a conversation at the gym, and I heard myself say, "I love back squats." As soon as I heard that come out of my mouth I thought, "No you don't. You do not love back squats. They hurt really bad, and they make you walk like a duck for a week." What I really meant was that I prefer back squats to other forms of self-inflicted torture.

We can mean all sorts of things when we use the word *love*. Perhaps that's why ancient Greek had several different words for love. The Scriptures are quite clear, though, about what agape means. First John 3:16 puts it very succinctly saying, "This is how we know love: Jesus laid down his life for us, and we ought to lay down our lives for our brothers and sisters." So: Want to know what love is? Look at Jesus. Look at the cross. Love is first and foremost sacrificial.

Growing in maturity is ultimately about learning to embrace a sacrificial way of life. *This* is really about *that*. Ultimately our journey forward, closing our maturity gap, isn't just about developing some privatized morality or simply experiencing a little bit better quality of life. No, no, no. It is way bigger and way better than that. It's about nothing less than embracing the loving, sacrificial way of life of the One who first loved us.

In fact, after listing out all of the virtues we have been exploring, the author of Second Peter tells us, plain and simple, why all of this really matters. In verse 8 he says to us, "If all these are yours and they're growing in you, they'll keep you from becoming inactive and unfruitful in the knowledge of our Lord Jesus Christ." Then in verse 10 he says that growing in maturity—becoming a fully functioning human being—is how you and I confirm our calling, or in a sense prove that the gospel is true and that Jesus is who he says he is. It is how we enter into the kingdom of our Lord and Savior Jesus Christ. Our journey forward isn't just about our own journey toward maturity, but it is about growing in our usefulness to the growth and expansion of the kingdom of God.

Love is behind, in the midst of, and out in front of all of this. Growing in love is how you and I experience the fullness of our life with God, and it is also how you and I partner with God in changing the world.

There is a moment in John's Gospel that I want us to zero in on. In chapter 13, Jesus is with his closest friends in Jerusalem just before the Passover. He is sharing a final meal with them before he is arrested and eventually crucified. Here is the passage:

> [1]Before the Festival of Passover, Jesus knew that his time had come to leave this world and go to the Father. Having loved his own who were in the world, he loved them fully.
>
> [2]Jesus and his disciples were sharing the evening meal. The devil had already provoked Judas, Simon Iscariot's son, to betray Jesus. [3]Jesus knew the Father had given everything into his hands and that he had come from God and was returning to God. [4]So he got up from the table and took off his robes. Picking up a linen towel, he tied it around his waist. [5]Then he poured water into a washbasin and began to wash the disciples' feet, drying them with the towel he was wearing. [6]When Jesus came to Simon Peter, Peter said to him, "Lord, are you going to wash my feet?"

⁷Jesus replied, "You don't understand what I'm doing now, but you will understand later."

⁸"No!" Peter said. "You will never wash my feet!"

Jesus replied, "Unless I wash you, you won't have a place with me."

⁹Simon Peter said, "Lord, not only my feet but also my hands and my head!"

¹⁰Jesus responded, "Those who have bathed need only to have their feet washed, because they are completely clean. You disciples are clean, but not every one of you." ¹¹He knew who would betray him. That's why he said, "Not every one of you is clean."

¹²After he washed the disciples' feet, he put on his robes and returned to his place at the table. He said to them, "Do you know what I've done for you? ¹³You call me 'Teacher' and 'Lord,' and you speak correctly, because I am. ¹⁴If I, your Lord and teacher, have washed your feet, you too must wash each other's feet. ¹⁵I have given you an example: Just as I have done, you also must do. ¹⁶I assure you, servants aren't greater than their master, nor are those who are sent greater than the one who sent them. ¹⁷Since you know these things, you will be happy if you do them. ¹⁸I'm not speaking about all of you. I know those whom I've chosen. But this is to fulfill the scripture, *The one who eats my bread has turned against me.*

¹⁹"I'm telling you this now, before it happens, so that when it does happen you will believe that I Am. ²⁰I assure you that whoever receives someone I send receives me, and whoever receives me receives the one who sent me."

The chapter begins by saying, "Having loved his own who were in the world, he loved them fully" (John 13:1). Another way to translate that last part is, "he now showed them the full extent of his love" (NIV, 1984). So whatever Jesus is about to do next is somehow going to reveal clearly what his love for the disciples looks like.

Starting in verse 4, the Gospel goes on to tell us that Jesus got up from the meal, took off his outer clothing, wrapped a towel around his waist, and began to wash his disciples' feet (John 13:4-11). This would have been shocking for the disciples. Washing someone's feet in the first century A.D. was a task reserved for servants. And here is Jesus, their rabbi, their teacher, their Messiah taking on the role of a servant and doing something for the disciples that they wouldn't even do for him.

What makes this even more shocking is what John tells us just before Jesus gets up and washes their feet. In verse 3, John says, "Jesus knew the Father had given everything into his hands and that he had come from God and was returning to God." So in this moment, Jesus knew that all power and authority had been given to him by God. He was well aware of his relationship with the Father, and what does Jesus do with all of that power and authority? He gets up, takes on the role of a servant, and washes the disciples' feet.

We can't miss this. By washing their feet, Jesus wasn't acting out of character as God in the flesh, and he wasn't laying aside power and authority. Instead, by washing the feet of those who would eventually deny and even betray him, Jesus was showing us what God's character and God's power actually look like.

Love in its truest sense is first and foremost sacrificial. It expresses itself in what it gives, and not what it gets. It lays aside its rights, it uses its power, its authority, its energy to lift others up. At the same time, this self-giving love is the very character of God, which means that it is what true power actually looks like.

The disciples, and especially Peter, had a really hard time with this. In fact, at first Peter refused to let Jesus do such a thing (John 13:6-8). That's because Jesus was the guy in charge. Jesus was the guy with the power and authority, and the guy with the power and the authority wouldn't do such a thing. It all seemed so upside down and backward.

True Power Looks Like Sacrificial Love

This wasn't the first time the disciples struggled to wrap their heads around what kind of Messiah Jesus was. As you read the Gospels, it is clear that the kingdom the disciples expected Jesus to usher in was quite different from the Kingdom Jesus was actually bringing. For instance, in Matthew 20, Jesus is with the disciples and he has just told them for at least the third time where all of this is eventually headed—not to a palace, but to the cross—and it isn't sinking in:

[17]As Jesus was going up to Jerusalem, he took the Twelve aside by themselves on the road. He told them, [18]"Look, we are

going up to Jerusalem. The Human One will be handed over to the chief priests and legal experts. They will condemn him to death. [19]They will hand him over to the Gentiles to be ridiculed, tortured, and crucified. But he will be raised on the third day."

[20]Then the mother of Zebedee's sons came to Jesus along with her sons. Bowing before him, she asked a favor of him.

[21]"What do you want?" he asked.

She responded, "Say that these two sons of mine will sit, one on your right hand and one on your left, in your kingdom."

[22]Jesus replied, "You don't know what you're asking! Can you drink from the cup that I'm about to drink from?"

They said to him, "We can."

[23]He said to them, "You will drink from my cup, but to sit at my right or left hand isn't mine to give. It belongs to those for whom my Father prepared it."

[24]Now when the other ten disciples heard about this, they became angry with the two brothers. [25]But Jesus called them over and said, "You know that those who rule the Gentiles show off their authority over them and their high-ranking officials order them around. [26]But that's not the way it will be with you. Whoever wants to be great among you will be your servant. [27]Whoever wants to be first among you will be your slave—[28]just as the Human One didn't come to be served but rather to serve and to give his life to liberate many people."

(Matthew 20:17-28)

Immediately after Jesus tells them of his death, two of his disciples, James and John, and their mother, come to Jesus. The mother wants to make a request on their behalf. What's really interesting is, if you connect the dots based on what we know from some of the other Gospels, this woman may also be Jesus' own aunt. It's sort of like when someone wins the lottery, and all of the relatives come out of the woodwork looking for a little bit to come their way. If she is Jesus' aunt, she's playing the relative card here. She asks a favor of Jesus: When he establishes his kingdom—takes care of all of their enemies, solves all of their problems, and sets up shop in the palace—would he allow her sons to sit at his right and his left? This is essentially the first-century way of asking Jesus if he would give her sons a promotion—put them in charge, give them a nice comfy spot right next to his throne in the fancy palace. When the other disciples see what's going on they get mad, not because she would have the audacity to ask Jesus such a thing, but because she beat them to it. Just more proof that we never really graduate from middle school.

Can you imagine how Jesus must have felt? "I've spent three years with you," he might have said. "I've shown you over and over again what my kingdom looks like, I just told you where all of this is headed—not to the palace, but to the cross. And you are arguing about who is going to get the corner office?"

You can't blame them. The disciples were just taking their cue from what they had experienced and how they knew that the world worked. For decades, they had been ruled by the Romans, which was the most powerful empire the world had ever seen. Rome was of course ruled by Caesar, who was in a sense worshiped as a god because he was able to bring a so-called peace to the world through military conquest.

In Matthew 20:25, Jesus describes the kind of power the kingdoms of the world use, saying they "show off their authority" over those they rule. It's a kind of power that comes from up above and pushes down. It's the kind of rule that overpowers and dominates. This is the sort of power that Rome wielded. If Caesar was going to demonstrate what his power looked like, he wouldn't wash a bunch of people's feet. He would have them crucified. When the disciples thought of power or what a ruler should look like, that kind of power is what they thought of because in their mind that's just how the world was.

Or should I say, that's just how the world is? We are familiar with this world, because it's the one we live in every single day. We live in a world where might makes right, where only the strong survive. When you think of the powerful—the important ones—who comes to mind? It's usually the rich, the successful, the beautiful, the famous. I mean, who makes the top ten lists in all of the tabloids? We live in a world of the haves and have-nots, and the haves are the ones running the show. The kingdom of the world places its trust in power over others, using force—in the form of money, fame, politics, or military—to rule over them and get what it wants.

It is estimated that globally the world spends around $1.6 trillion per year on warfare. Let me show you what 1.6 trillion looks like:

1,600,000,000,000

That's a whole lot of zeros. What's perhaps even more shocking is that just ten percent of that amount would be enough to fund the global initiatives established by the members of the United Nations aimed at ending global poverty and hunger by the year 2030.[1] Look at that military spending and tell me: What sort of power does the world place its trust in? The kind of power that rules through force and domination. How does that seem to be working out for us? It doesn't seem to be bringing about a whole lot of change, at least not the kind of change that sticks around for very long.

True power, the kind of power that brings about lasting change, doesn't look like Caesar crushing all those who stand in his way. True power looks like Jesus, the Lord of lords, washing the feet of those who will soon turn their backs on him. True power looks like agape love.

I recently read a reflection that Napoleon Bonaparte gave about Christ while he was in exile on the island of Saint Helena. Napoleon, of course, is remembered as one of the great military leaders of all time. What is fascinating, though, is that as Napoleon reflected on his life and compared his accomplishments to other conquerors like Caesar and Alexander the Great, he recognized that Jesus was actually the greatest conqueror of all time. Jesus, he recognized, won over the devotion of the whole human race. While great men like himself and other rulers are forgotten after their time, Jesus is proclaimed, loved, and even worshiped throughout the whole world many centuries after his death.

Wow. A man who conquered a large portion of the known world through force recognized that the power he used pales in comparison to the power that Christ demonstrated. And how does Christ capture the hearts of people? Not by force, but by loving them, serving them, and giving his life for them. The kind of power that creates change that will last is the power that is demonstrated through self-giving love.

Remember, our maturity isn't just about us and our own personal and private life. The result of our maturity is that we become the kind of people who partner with God in ushering in the kingdom of heaven. And love is how we do that.

Love Is Our Future

In Paul's famous chapter on love, 1 Corinthians 13, he speaks of love as a sort of bridge that somehow brings God's future, when all of creation will be renewed, into the present. After the part of the chapter you typically hear read at weddings, Paul says, "Love never fails. As for prophecies, they will be brought to an end. As for tongues, they will stop. As for knowledge, it will be brought to an end. We know in part and we prophesy in part; but when the perfect comes, what is partial will be brought to an end" (1 Corinthians 13:8-10). We are currently living in the time of "now but not yet." Christ's resurrection has launched the beginning of God's new world right here in the midst of this one, and one day Jesus will return to finish what was started. In other words, the completeness will come.

Paul finishes this passage by saying, "Now faith, hope, and love remain—these three things—and the greatest of these is love" (1 Corinthians 13:13). In the present we have three tools that help to orient ourselves around God's promised future: faith, hope, and love. And the greatest is love. See, when completion comes, when heaven and earth are joined together and everything is set right, faith and hope will be realized and as a result they will no longer be necessary. Love, however, will remain because, as N. T. Wright says, "Love is the way of life in the new world to which, by grace, we are bound. We need to learn it here and now. It is the grammar of the language we shall speak there. The more progress we make in it here, the better we shall be equipped."[2] Love is not only about you and me moving forward in our journey toward completion and wholeness. It is also how we partner with God in moving the redemptive plan for all of creation forward. Love is the goal of it all, the basic characteristic of the redeemed world.

I can imagine that all of us, in some way, want to see things change. We have a sense that the world doesn't have to be the way it is, and we want things to be different. How do you suppose that change is going to happen? I wonder how different our world would look if those of us who identified as Jesus followers actually followed Jesus' lead and truly embraced a loving, sacrificial way of life.

In every way, Jesus and the kingdom of God stand in complete opposition to the kingdom of the world. In Matthew's Gospel, the squabble among the disciples over who was the greatest is sandwiched between two descriptions of Jesus' sacrificial death (Matthew 20: 17-19, 28). That means that where the kingdom of the world looks like people pushing each other down in order to lift themselves up, the kingdom of God looks like Jesus on the cross giving his life for a bunch of people who don't deserve it. The kingdom of the world demonstrates power over, but the kingdom of God demonstrates power under—it uses its authority, its very life, to lift others up. Wherever people allow the radical love of God to heal them and the character of Christ to be formed in them—wherever this selfless love is being used to serve and lift others up—that's where the kingdom of God is, and that's where the kingdom of God is advancing.

At first this seems backward and upside down. But those of us who truly enter into this radical kingdom and take on this worldview soon realize that the kingdom of God isn't what's upside down. This world is what is upside down, and Jesus came to flip it right side up.

In Matthew 16:24, Jesus says, "All who want to come after me must say no to themselves, take up their cross, and follow me." Taking up one's cross isn't just about bearing up under some sort of difficult circumstance. Sometimes you'll hear people talk about taking up their cross after they get a flat tire on their way to work. That's not taking up your cross. The cross is the demonstration of what God was willing to do in order to rescue a broken world that God loves. Taking up our cross is about identifying a broken place in the world and partnering with God in putting the pieces back together, because we love as God loves.

Jesus goes on to say in the next verse, "All who want to save their lives will lose them. But all who lose their lives because of me will find them" (Matthew 16:25). In other words, if you want to find your life you have to give it away. Taking on this posture—serving—isn't so much an obligation as it is an opportunity. This sort of service-oriented love is where real, abundant life is found.

Years ago when I was serving as a youth pastor, I took a group of students on a mission to trip to Jamaica. Most of us know Jamaica for all of its resorts, but when you get outside of their walls you discover that Jamaica is in fact an impoverished nation. One of our days there was spent at what they call the infirmary. It is essentially a concrete open-air bunker with rows of beds that serves as a sort of hospice care. The people who are at the infirmary have been forgotten by everyone they've ever known and literally left there to die.

I was really nervous about taking a bunch of privileged suburban kids to a place like this, because I thought it would be way too uncomfortable for them. I was worried that they would hate it. Truth is, I knew it was going to be really uncomfortable for *me*, and I thought *I* was going to hate it.

When we got there, though, I was blown away by how the students gave themselves to those people. They sat on the ends of the beds and rubbed lotion on the patients' hands and feet. They fed them and helped to change their bandages. They asked them about their lives and listened to their stories.

When we got back to camp the kids were electric. They couldn't stop talking about how rich the experience was for them. I remember one of them saying, "This is the closest I have ever felt to God."

You see, we are never closer to God than when we are demonstrating God's character—when we are demonstrating and practicing true love. Jesus comes to each of us and says, "Come follow me; let me show you who you really are. You want to experience real life? Then you have to give it away." Jesus both teaches and demonstrates that love, the epitome of spiritual maturity, is first and foremost sacrificial.

In wrapping all of this up, let me ask you this: If real love is sacrificial, what is love costing you?

I've heard it said that the kingdom of God grows where you and I choose to bleed. Where are you bleeding? How are you taking up your cross?

This is a hard question for me. My wife and I were having a really honest conversation about this just the other day. Very early in our relationship there were some obvious and intentional ways in which our commitment to the kingdom of God was costing us. It involved sacrifice. It was an intrusion on our lives, and we loved it. It was difficult, it was uncomfortable, it involved sacrifice, but it was so worth it. But as we started to look around at our lives now, we weren't able to identify as easily how our commitment to the kingdom of God was costing us. Yeah, sure we tithe, and we go to church (as a pastor I kind of have to), we read our Bibles, and we try to be nice to people. But that's really about it. There's not any sort of sacrifice that disrupts our lives. We seem way too comfortable. Don't get me wrong: The goal isn't just to be uncomfortable. It's to make an impact for the kingdom. But it can be so easy to get married, have some kids, and settle into a routine. Slowly but surely, you start to see your home as a fortress and your time, energy, and resources as something to be protected instead of something to be used in order to lift others up. Somehow we have become safe, and the kingdom of God isn't safe. If love is sacrificial, what is it costing me? Perhaps this is a clue for me about where I need to do some work to move forward.

What about you?

In Your Group

Study John 13:1-20

Read John 13:1-20 on the following page, paying attention to Jesus' actions and how they demonstrate agape love. Consider the following questions as you read the passage, and answer them in the space provided:

1. What do you want to know more about as you read this passage?
2. How do you think Jesus' disciples felt while Jesus washed their feet? How would you have felt?
3. What is the relationship between Jesus' knowledge and love (see verse 3)?
4. What about this passage encourages you or challenges you?
5. What other virtues from 2 Peter 1:5-7 do you see at work in this passage? What is the relationship between them? What role does love play?

John 13:1-20

¹Before the Festival of Passover, Jesus knew that his time had come to leave this world and go to the Father. Having loved his own who were in the world, he loved them fully.

²Jesus and his disciples were sharing the evening meal. The devil had already provoked Judas, Simon Iscariot's son, to betray Jesus. ³Jesus knew the Father had given everything into his hands and that he had come from God and was returning to God. ⁴So he got up from the table and took off his robes. Picking up a linen towel, he tied it around his waist. ⁵Then he poured water into a washbasin and began to wash the disciples' feet, drying them with the towel he was wearing. ⁶When Jesus came to Simon Peter, Peter said to him, "Lord, are you going to wash my feet?"

⁷Jesus replied, "You don't understand what I'm doing now, but you will understand later."

⁸"No!" Peter said. "You will never wash my feet!"

Jesus replied, "Unless I wash you, you won't have a place with me."

⁹Simon Peter said, "Lord, not only my feet but also my hands and my head!"

¹⁰Jesus responded, "Those who have bathed need only to have their feet washed, because they are completely clean. You disciples are clean, but not every one of you." ¹¹He knew who would betray him. That's why he said, "Not every one of you is clean."

¹²After he washed the disciples' feet, he put on his robes and returned to his place at the table. He said to them, "Do you know what I've done for you? ¹³You call me 'Teacher' and 'Lord,' and you speak correctly, because I am. ¹⁴If I, your Lord and teacher, have washed your feet, you too must wash each other's feet. ¹⁵I have given you an example: Just as I have done, you also must do. ¹⁶I assure you, servants aren't greater than their master, nor are those who are sent greater than the one who sent them. ¹⁷Since you know these things, you will be happy if you do them.

[18]I'm not speaking about all of you. I know those whom I've chosen. But this is to fulfill the scripture, *The one who eats my bread has turned against me.*

[19]"I'm telling you this now, before it happens, so that when it does happen you will believe that I Am. [20]I assure you that whoever receives someone I send receives me, and whoever receives me receives the one who sent me."

What Resonates With You?

What from this session resonates with you? How does the reflection on love encourage you, and how does it challenge you?

What encouraged you?

What challenged you?

Agape Love

In your own words, define what agape love is in the space below. Describe how it differs from what we mean most of the time when we use the English word *love*. Then list as many examples as you can think of that indicate agape love that you have experienced or witnessed.

Upside-Down Power

In your own experience, how is the kingdom of the world different from the kingdom of God? Draw or describe what comes to mind when you think of worldly power in the space below. Then add to your drawing or description to illustrate how the kingdom of God shows true power or brings about change.

How have you experienced and/or witnessed the upside-down power of love? In the space provided, name at least one time when you have experienced love in a radical, unexpected, upside-down way. Then list a time when you have shown love to someone else in this upside-down manner. What power did you feel in those instances? How does it inspire you to love going forward?

Forward Goals

How can you and your fellow small group members push one another forward when it comes to supplementing your faith with love? This will have a lot to do with how you want to be able to answer the questions on page 147—"What is love costing you? Where are you bleeding? How are you taking up your cross?" Use the space below to think of answers to these questions, and formulate practical, specific goals for moving forward in love. Be sure also to identify how you and your group members will hold one another accountable and push one another forward.

What goals will help you move toward the virtue of love?

Conclusion

Now that you have completed this final session, I want to finish with a story. I have a friend who is a pharmacist down in Miami. I know, tough gig, right? He is the biggest LeBron James fan on the planet. He has the shoes, the jersey, the bobblehead doll. When Lebron James played for the Miami Heat, my friend would buy season tickets right behind the players' bench. I mean, we are talking the best seats in the house.

One day my friend was at this really exclusive gym playing basketball, when in walked in Lebron James himself along with a couple other Heat players. It was during the off-season, and they were there to play a little pick-up game. When they walked in, my friend's jaw hit the floor. Then Lebron actually walked up to him and said that they still need one guy to play. He asked if he wanted to be on his team. My friend said he was speechless. He literally couldn't get his mouth to work. What would you have done?

You know what my friend did? He told LeBron no. Seriously, he got so nervous and even scared about the thought of playing with this guy he had idolized that he chickened out. Get this: He told him that he couldn't stay and play because he had to go let his dog out. Can you imagine what LeBron was thinking? "Really, you're wearing my jersey right now and you can't stay and play with me because you have to go and let your dog out?" Ridiculous, right?

Now, the first thing you need to know about that story is that it never happened. I made the whole thing up. Pretty impressive, right?

The second thing you need to know is that it happens all the time. Just replace King James with King Jesus. So many of us are huge Jesus fans, and we sign up for front-row seats—we go to church, we give, we study. But Jesus invites us to be more than just fans. Jesus is standing right there beside us, asking if we want to play the game with him.

There is a difference between being a fan and actually playing the game. The same goes with following Jesus. He does not invite us just to believe in who he is and what he has done. He calls us out of the stands and empowers us to play an integral part in what he is doing. That's essentially what this maturity thing is all about. This is what it means to move forward in our life of faith—it is to do what Jesus does.

Perhaps the most incredible thing is that Jesus actually thinks you can do it. In Jesus, God has given us everything we need to live a really beautiful life. The question is, will we take God up on it?

Remember, in life there is no neutral. We are all headed somewhere, and we are all becoming someone. The question is, are we headed where we want to go and becoming who we want to be? My hope for you is that the Forward Goals you have set will empower you to answer "yes" to that question. My desire is that you will find strength in others on the same journey, that you will discover yourselves pushing one another forward so that you can be more than what you have thought possible. My prayer for you is that you will fully embrace what has been made available to you in Jesus Christ and that you will accept his invitation to live a life of forward movement toward the Kingdom.

Endnotes

Introduction

1. *One: A Small Group Journey Toward Life-Changing Community*, by Nick Cunningham with Trevor Miller (Abingdon Press, 2016). Participant book, leader guide, and DVD.

Session 1: Goodness

1. *The Early Christian Letters for Everyone: James, Peter, John, and Judah*, by N. T. Wright (Westminster John Knox, 2011), pages 102-103.

Session 3: Self-Control

1. *The Spirit of the Disciplines: Understanding How God Changes Lives*, by Dallas Willard (HarperCollins, 1988), page 77.

Session 4: Perseverance

1. *The NIV Application Commentary, 2 Peter, Jude*, by Douglas J. Moo (Zondervan, 1997), pages 50-51.

2. Perseverance; https://www.merriam-webster.com/dictionary/perseverance.

3. *The Exegetical Dictionary of the New Testament*, Volume 3, edited by Horst Balz and Gerhard M. Schneider (Eerdmans, 2003), page 405.

4. *Beyond Good and Evil*, by Friedrich Nietzsche, translated by Helen Zimmern (London: 1907, sec. 188). Quoted in *A Long Obedience in the Same Direction*, by Eugene H. Peterson (20th Anniversary Edition; InterVarsity Press, 2000), page 17.

5. *Outliers: The Story of Success*, by Malcolm Gladwell (Little, Brown, and Company, 2008), page 39.

6. *The Epistle of Paul to the Philippians: An Introduction and Commentary*, by Ralph P. Martin (Eerdmans, 1987), page 80.

7. Ibid., page 81.

Session 5: Godliness

1. *The Pastoral Epistles*, by George W. Knight III (Grand Rapids MI: Eerdmans, 1992, page 197). Quoted in *1-2 Timothy and Titus: To Guard the Deposit*, by R. Kent Hughes and Bryan Chapell (Preaching the Word; Crossway, 2012), page 113.

Session 6: Mutual Affection

1. *The Weight of Glory*, by C. S. Lewis (HarperCollins paperback edition; HarperCollins, 2001), page 46.

Session 7: Love

1. "Just ten percent of world military spending could knock off poverty: think tank," by Belinda Goldsmith for Reuters, April 2016. http://www.reuters.com/article/us-global-military-goals-idUSKCN0X12EQ. Accessed December 16, 2016. See also http://www.un.org/sustainabledevelopment/poverty/.

2. *Paul for Everyone: 1 Corinthians*, by N. T. Wright (Westminster John Knox, 2004), page 177.